Kentucky Review
2015

Editor-in-Chief
Robert S. King

Associate Editors
Joan Colby, Helen Losse, Mike James, Ken Craft,
Marie Lecrivain, Sara Clancy, Lee Passarella

Assistant Editor
Rachel L. MacAulay

Design and Production
Diane Kistner

www.kentuckyreview.net

A Good Works Project

ISSN 2376-9920 (print)
ISSN 2376-9939 (online)

Cover artwork, "Horse," by Franz Lechner
Cover and interior book design by Diane Kistner
Georgia text with Insignia titling

Published by Kentucky Review (a division of FutureCycle Press)
Lexington, Kentucky, USA

ISSN 2376-9920
ISBN 978-1-938853-94-4

ABOUT THIS ISSUE

WELCOME to a huge publication! During its second year, *Kentucky Review* attracted so much good work from so many good writers and poets that we have compiled a print edition of more than 300 pages.

Unlike the 2014 issue, KR 2015 contains flash fiction as well as poetry. Rather than group the work by genre, we have opted instead to showcase the authors in alphabetical order by last name. Some writers have both flash fiction and poetry in this issue.

Because printing costs rise as page counts rise, we had to shorten the author bios included at the end of the print edition. However, on our website you can find both longer bios and photos of the writers, links to their personal websites and blogs, and even some videos of them reading their work. Visit kentuckyreview.net and click on "Issues." While we don't separate flash fiction from poetry in the print edition, we do so on the website.

As always, I thank all of the editors of *Kentucky Review* (see the title page) and also Diane Kistner, the Director of FutureCycle Press, who designs and publishes KR. We are proud that KR is one of the press's Good Works projects, with all proceeds from sales benefitting Action Against Hunger.

Of course, I thank all our readers and contributors and trust that everyone will find a lot to like in these pages.

—Robert S. King, Editor-in-Chief

IN THIS ISSUE

Barriers

The brush rattles—
the way death sounds

in my grandmother's rattled
throat.

A doe and two fawn
walk by so close

that if I open the window
I could brush them

with my fingers. But—
I don't bother,

and the deer cross
the clearing.

Glass between us.
The small barrier

I press my forehead against.

In the morning, I know a hunter
will reach into the field,

and my grandmother's coffin
will hold her like a new dress.

Desaparecido

Mexico says 22,322 people now "disappeared."
—Al Jazeera (22 Aug. 2014)

Was the motive profit, revenge? A debt unpaid?
Perhaps nothing at all beyond the chance snub,
a random curse. After they took you away,
silence thickened.

I remained to answer the phone, ear cocked
for footsteps and paced, glass shards scuffing the wood
beneath my heels. Your towel dried in the bathroom.
Strands of your hair threaded the drain.
I retrieved a shirt flung to the floor in their haste.

Neighbors no longer speak your name.
Life, like a bolt of silk ripped down the middle,
holds no promise. No urn, no grave. I thank God for that.

Days limp. Your car, covered with dust, haunts
the driveway. No bread rises in the kitchen.
The clocks clamor. I lie in bed, wrapped in your shirt,
seek comfort in the ripple of vowels,
rustle of consonants— as I chant:
regresarás, regresarás, regresarás...

Inventory

Between the two of us we manage to hold on to almost
all we need to know. You keep track of 27 bridge conventions,
the formula for converting centigrade to Fahrenheit, shortcuts,
losses, how to light my pilot, change a tire.

I get to remember our first date, the kids' close calls, the lyrics
to *Oklahoma,* my mother's grip on my elbow, the words in French
for "Where is the bathroom?," how not to change a tire. Along
with recollections of sand, hot beneath bare feet, odor of ozone

after lightning storms, a stranger's compliment, a squabble
in a parking lot, our battalion of etceteras thrives, takes up residency
in the back yard. It lays down roots. Like bamboo that burrows
beneath the house, loosens tiles on the kitchen floor, reappears

in the bedroom, it survives, barring dementia or demise. I'd like
to believe that once we're gone we'll leave behind some memories
of ourselves lined up in rows like visitors' shoes outside a temple door.

Sink

It glows grey and sends up murky flares. It awaits
My audience. It emits its *confuses paroles*.
I listen, dig deep without gloves, asking Darwin
If this is the place where the tadpole sprouted legs,
But in this mush of last night's leeks and rice, this muck
Originates from a deeper place where monsters
Blink back at me patiently in the shadowy
Waters. A plunger shoved vigorously unclogs,
But the thing in the deep, even though I scour the
Gleaming aluminum, waits lower until dusk
For me to acknowledge. It lingers Loch-Ness-like
Until I answer its demands, feed it, make it
Lap dog, admit it's mine, admit it's me, forget self,
Remember it alone until it turns the tap.

The Victorious Christian Couple

The members of the victorious Christian couple
Attend church together, and after the last "amen," they
Take long strolls in parks where the leaves are leaping
Off the branches, committing suicide, but they each
Call this autumn, not a mass cult exodus, nothing to take
Personally. When they start talking at the same time, each says,
"No, you first," laughing delicately as the wind picks up.
They sigh at the gravel path, hold hands passionately, stewing
The rest for later: "Do not open until marriage" is written
On a gift tag stitched to the woman's brassiere of ribbon
And egg shell crepe paper with matching egg shell panties,
And the man's white cotton boxers are padlocked and alarmed.
They don't even call this a date until they have set a date.
Much remains unspoken, except in silent prayer. To forget,
They discuss everything else they can think of except "it."

The members of the victorious Christian couple
Worry less than the defeated couple making out on
The park bench they pass—those two have only locked
Tongues to be sure that the other one doesn't wander off
Again, are stroking each other on parts that would hurt
If somebody squeezed them hard and shouted, "You
Can't leave me yet! Not until I say so!"—but let's be
Honest. Those two who do it to Snoop Doggy Dogg
Duets, with woofs and scratches, slaps and pap smears,
Their clothes don't smell as clean, but their jokes are
Funnier, with more pain in them, the ideas they scream out
Sound more original—sin always seems like innovation
At first, until things end the same old way—and if these couples
Left the park at the exact same moment, the benched sinners
Might cross into incoming traffic just for the adrenaline rush of it.

Are They Boulders

or whales that breached
this mountain peak millennia ago,
rising out of the dirt as if through water
to be transfixed by stars?

       What unknowable
events have passed their stony gazes?

When will they shake off
the oaks that harpoon their mossy backs,
barnacled with galax and heuchera
and fern?
       When will they dive
back under, taking with them everything
we recognize?

At Stouchsburg Cemetery

The wall, flint stacked like volumes
in the book of ages, crumbles now,
exposing to light rock laid to rest in darkness
two centuries ago. And the tombstones,
washed by acid rain until the words
have smoothed to the occasional
stuttered syllable and moss makes its home
in ancestors' names. What does it
matter? Who cares about the long-dead
except the deeply sad, and we're hoping
to get over it, to wake tomorrow
lit with ease like newborns.

Or at least to get on with it,
to rise and dress and utter whatever
syllables the day requires, all the while
praying something will fall on us,
hard and heavy, and knock us
cockeyed with happiness.

Country Man

for Colan

My neighbor still drives, though when he exits
the Farm and Convenience with a carton of cigarettes
he has to stumble into the car door to stop himself. *It's a bitch
getting old,* I say. *I ain't there yet,* he replies.

He's run off every woman who would've cared
for him, sits inside his little house smoking
alone. *There's something attractive about him,*
a friend who knows him says. *He's still got the devil*

in his eye. He used to have the devil in his fingertips,
played his banjo as if it were that or go to hell. One good
stroke put an end to his picking. Now this new demon,
Parkinson's, plucks on his nerves. He'll tell you he's not the kind

to be spoon-fed and diapered. When his hands
start to shake too much to light a Winston, I'll see
his mailbox overspill, know he's put himself down
like he did his old blind hound last year.

Photograph: Burlap #2

The ripped threads are only burlap
and nothing else, green and bronze strands
that glow in the peach light of an October dawn.
They don't mean anything by their frailty,
didn't ask to be teased out of the larger scene
of two wooden tobacco wagons with burlap sides,
hitched to a tractor and driven on bald tires
to the edge of the neighbor's waiting field.
Yet, in this light, all is art, camera fodder.
This early, nothing about the day has frayed,
though there exists always the possibility.

The cries of stray birds, the only sounds
on this cold morning. Later, a phone ringing,
someone you love who tells you someone else
you love rose at dawn like you, tried to stand
but collapsed, dragging the night's warm blankets,
faded with years, to the floor. But you aren't yet
at that part of the story. You're still in the field,
bent low to photograph the shredded burlap,
the dazzle of light at its tasseled ends.

Driving My Aunt Back from the Nursing Home Where We Visited Her Sister

Do you know how to get there?
She means her house this time. I point
to a brick farmhouse two centuries old,
three wooden sheds tilted aslant out back,
tell her, *I went to an auction there once*
with Uncle Elwood. It rained like crazy.
I held an umbrella for him while he drank
his coffee. I told her the same thing
on the way over. She says, *He wasn't supposed*
to have it, and I'm pleased she remembers
her husband of sixty years, his tricky heart.

Do you know how to get there? I don't,
and I've lived here all my life. A bewildered
sigh. Gone, the maps for roads she's traveled
for ninety years, the word for the stubble
in this field we're passing, the name for the snow
sifted like powdered sugar over the dark dirt,
for the birds that rise from the field,
five hundred at least, a sight so astonishing
I want to stop and open the windows
to hear the rush of wind tugged by their wings,
to breathe this February air. *Geese,* I tell her,
look at all the geese.

Visiting Her Sister at the Nursing Home

I lead my aunt through a sliding double door
that startles with its whoosh and glide. Around
a corner to face a corridor she stares down
as if she's a shipmate on Franklin's doomed trek
across the Arctic. At the hallway's end, elevators
that will take us to the third floor. But first
the trudge along white tiles whose waxed shine
blinds like sunlight on ice. Her pace, glacial.
From a few feet ahead, I call encouragements
over my shoulder. If I walk beside her
she freezes: no map for the journey,
no guide, lost in the wasteland.

Her Legacy

She had no use for women,
for daughters or granddaughters,
saved her stingy love
for the sons who died too young,
the son-in-law who deserted,
the grandsons who stampeded
through her house, then vanished
into other women's lives.

But the women of her line
carry her in whip-thin bodies,
in their nervous hands that never
know stillness, in mountain-women's
cheeks, skin taut over bone
as the thin layer of soil stretched
over Blue Ridge granite. In eyes pale
as creek water. In the twang
of a mandolin's string that threads
through their voices. In the curve
of the spine that testifies
that whatever they do will never
satisfy, never be enough.

Honeymoon

We're so young we don't have a clue
how to be married or what to do
to turn on the hulking black furnace
in the mountain cabin my aunt and uncle
loaned us for our no-money honeymoon.

We layer long johns under our look-alike
flannel shirts and faded jeans,
huddle all the rainy day under blankets
on the top of the two bunk beds
we've pushed together in one of the spartan
rooms. I pretend to read *Don Quixote*;
you lie close, stroking my shoulder and hair.

Strange to be alone so long, strange to sleep
with another body struggling toward the center
of the narrow bed. Gradually we'll wear
sharp angles down until they fit
but just now everything about us is new,
like birthday presents with the wrapping just off,
like the bright edges of unused tools.

BOBBY STEVE BAKER

Pioneering Solo Female Country Music Star

Cousin Emmy (Cynthia May Carver)

gimme an audience
I go on stage and there's not a dull moment
I don't script anything this is who I am
Cousin Emmy and I'm a live wire
been playing this banjo
since I was a baby in Barren County
I'll frail and drop thumb so fast and true
I'll blow the boys right off the stage
and that's the unexaggerated truth
I sing I dance tell jokes
one time I pulled a harmonica
right outta my cleavage
didn't have anywhere else to put it
got a good laugh though
in my show I aim to please
if you like it
tell everybody you know
if you don't like it well
there's somethin wrong with you
just hush up and go on home
I betcha your hummin
Ruby are You Mad at Your Man
before you get there
I'll tell though Buddy it takes more than talent to be a star
you gotta be willin to put in the miles
some days between WHAS and playin live
I'd drive five hundred miles
hey that's kinda catchy
there's a song there
I'm gonna write that down
Ruby now that song put me on the map
those Osborne boys
God bless 'em they recorded it

they're top-o-the-chart Bluegrass musicians and connected
they play all the big festivals and sell records by the thousands
Ruby just hits Bluegrass right in the belly of the groove
now everybody's recorded it
when the 60's came along
they told me *Emmy country music's comin back!*
shoot I didn't know it went anywhere
I stayed busy being Cousin Emmy
even got in the movies
moved to California but I ain't the Beverly Hillbillies
I'm Cousin Emmy

Renoir Paints My Husband and Me at Breakfast in Cagnes-Sur-Mer

> *To let the world know after our time that we were here,*
> *and that we loved. —Renoir*

My husband marvels at the artist's accomplishment,
his brush fat with alizarin crimson, adding a touch
of pigment to the apples. The still life of our table:
linens scented with sun, their creases, violet-hued
white plates and cups, a pitcher of café au lait,
frothy foam spilling from dark roast,
two rustic Chanticleer apples sweet and ripe,
warm in chrome yellow, smoky glaze of red-blue,
redolent of earth's loamy richness.

I pour the café, pass the wicker basket
of *pains aux chocolat* studded with nuggets of cocoa butter,
flaky layers of pastry where my love, a smile on his face,
still leans toward me these many years,

this warm September where even now
the sky doubles itself in the Bay d'Antibes, and he dabs
at the goodness dribbling down my chin,
my eyes closed to the sun.

ROY BENTLEY

Photograph Taken in a Basement in Ohio

My grandmother Potter drapes a grey blouse over a wire coat hanger.
Work she has accomplished with a degree of skill. Work that pains her.
Work she donates without promise of recompense or benefit or gratitude.
Now, may she know if there is a merciful God and the answer be *There is*.
May she forget the indenture of cooking and cleaning, washing and ironing.
May one of the ranch houses of one of her children in Kentucky or Virginia
or Ohio be home, if only in memory. May she never again count currency
from a safety-pinned stash in a brassiere; if she does, may she find those
handkerchief-secreted ones fives tens twenties infinite and inexhaustible.
May she believe the best about her dreamland-heaven and be proven right.
May she find horehound hard candy. Luden Brothers cherry cough drops.
May the black dog awakening at her feet be named Snowball, her favorite.
May she never forget the steam rising from outhouses on winter mornings,
the sepia slouching of row houses. May she feel love in the new republic.

You'll Never Leave Harlan Alive

Once in Florida when I was young and my friends were young too,
a good friend of mine died. But before he did, he came to my house
and we drank that peat-smoked scotch we both liked then, the ice
and glass tumblers refracting a warm white light. I played him
Kathy Mattea's uber-twangy "You'll Never Leave Harlan Alive."
I was about to refill his glass. The wind outside was howling,
an outrageous rainfall into its third hour of coming down.
Some stories just sound better if you're liquored up, too.
Like the one where he gave an unlucky foe a "curbie"—
said he rested the downed opponent's propped-open mouth
against a concrete curbstone. Kicked his head. From behind.
Like gravestones displaying angels, multiple points of view
exist as to what constitutes one. He talked through the song,
saying Lee Marvin was drunk on the set of *The Professionals,*
a Western about friends and enemies, unscrupulous behavior
on the Road to Riches. He said he was a star, Lee Marvin.
Told me there was dynamite in the movie. Explosions.
He said Burt Lancaster, as the dynamiter, was no angel.
He had me at the word *Western.* Do I need to say we each
got a kick out of the other, that the deluge then stopped?
Do I have to spell it out, the way his laughter bested mine,
and was more heartfelt? We teehee-ed like schoolgirls.
Young as we were, we understood "Dynamite, not faith,
will move that mountain into this pass. Peace, brother."
Maybe it sounded much too true to be ignored, and maybe
we were ignoring truth in favor of what we *wanted* to be true.
Like that the person sitting in front of you, and laughing,
will never die and make a sound like smothering a fuse.

Michael Jordan Slippers: A Modern Cinderella

Her dark arms pour from a sleeveless silver sequined-dress
She's in position: bent knees, on the balls of her feet

Hair down like church
Michael Jordan slippers: a modern Cinderella

She dominates the paint
This gym floor turned dance ball, turned club

She ballerina spins: pure college prospect
She jukes one way, breaks the boys' ankles

Pumps her shoulders with the rhythm of the crowd
They're a wave pool of children in a half-court game

Her ceramic smile breaks into thin slices of moon
The disco ball tosses puzzle pieces of light off the backboard

She, the tall girl, the power forward, grinds with the smallest boy in the room
Her infatuation trapped in his sweat beads

But he can't hold her, it's not his fault
Her father is the only man who was ever able to block her jump shot.

Pound for Pound

JUST KILLING TIME. Just moving through the day. Just too hot. Just too thirsty so I went into a bodega, Avenue B and 5th, bought a beer. Behind the register a hard-looking guy, Boricua maybe, gray in his rough beard, hair cut short, eyes sleepy-hard. Behind him fight posters and fight pictures under the shelves stocked with cold medicines, sore throat medicines, Alka-Seltzer, Trojans with the warrior-helmet logo. Some of the photographs autographed. I recognized some of the fighters. In one photo young Mike Tyson, "Best of luck" in cursive and his signature. He looked young, before he got in trouble, when he was moving up and undefeated. I put the bottle of Bud on the counter.

"Good day for a cold *cerveza*," the man said.

"Yes it is."

I gave him a five.

"Been sweating my ass off all day. All fucking summer and now this. These fans don't do nothing after a while. Blow the hot air around. Indian Summer. That what they call it, right?"

"Right," I said.

"Fuck those Indians."

He pressed down the keys on the old register, made change.

"You see this picture here. Ali versus Frazier in Manila. Over one hundred degrees and they go at it fourteen rounds before Frazier quits. None of that twelve-round bullshit they got now. Over one hundred degrees, man. So what am I complaining? Right?"

"You can complain."

"What the fuck, right? You right, man. I can complain. Fuck it. I hate this New York shit. Not a fucking break and then bang, it be winter time and you freeze your fucking ass off."

He put the beer in a bag, twisted the paper tight at top, easier to drink.

"You like the fights?" he said.

"I watch them sometimes on TV."

"Who you like? Today. Who your favorite?"

"Ward. I like Andre Ward."

"They say he going to be the next pound-for-pound best. I don't like that shit. Pound for pound. That shit's bullshit, man. How you going to tell if a guy at lightweight going to beat a middleweight or a heavyweight if he weighed that much? They be a different fighter with each weight. At welterweight the best welterweight be the best welterweight.

How come that not good enough? We don't need to go into all that pound-for-pound shit. Andre Ward, man. I like him too. He smart. He the smartest fucking fighter fighting."

"He makes everyone else look stupid."

"You right, man. He beat them with his brain first."

He pointed to a photograph of Roberto Duran. Duran had his hands in the air and someone was placing a belt around his waist. Duran was smiling, but he wasn't looking at the camera.

"That's my man. A young Duran. Before he got fat like a fucking pig. *Manos de piedre*. Hands of stone. They say he hit you with a little tap you still feeling it the next week."

"I saw him running in the park once."

"Here?"

"In Central Park."

"No shit. How he look?"

"He looked like an old man."

"Like a fat fuck, right? When you see him?"

"When I first moved here."

"No shit. He fought too long. He should have stopped at lightweight. Or when he fucked up Davey Moore. Then he should have said fuck it and walked away. But he got fat like a pig and kept fighting for the money. Fuck the money. The glory. The legacy, man. That should come first. You win the belt, no one ever take that shit away from you. Never."

"That must be nice."

"I bet that be the best feeling in the world. The champ. So fuck it if Duran look like a fat pig now, right? He always be the champ."

"Forever."

"Forever, man. Forever."

"Stay cool."

"You too, man. You stay cool. Like Andre Ward in the ring, right?"

"Right."

I walked out of the bodega, twisted the cap, drank down some beer. I made a muscle for me.

"In this corner," I said.

Retreat/Return

after reading about Jetsunma Tenzin Palmo

What winds what waters snow and silent wars
twelve years in a Himalayan cave. Keening years,

sequestered. Eat snow.
Let blood flow free at open thighs, lotus

undisturbed. Kneel to hear a word
from mountain, rumors from the core.

Believe at times
that you make bloom societies of stainless cloud.

Wail before the floods in spring. Awful plunge
of winter, aging. Tortured wisdom of a naked place,

the wind its only instrument. Each season's purpose.
Lose your words and learn from all of this.

What would tell you it's the day you may
or must return, shelter in the city,

plumb-line broken? Become, then, a nun
to everything untempered. Hunger with the beasts

and wear the damage gracefully. Drip a little water
on a sun-scorched worm who calculated badly distance

from the concrete to the grass.
Find a safer place for him in dirt. Know

that it's absurd to break out all our silver
when the world is aching for a place to sleep.

In pencil write out poems of the music on the backs
of fragile things. Tell no one how you heard them.

Let them go unpublished, soft expressions
of the breath's slow return to the unknowing, known.

Not King at All (Dream Poem #32)

"And when you leave the world you have already received the truth in the images." —Gospel of Philip

My dreams don't tend to kings but how your lonesome tides
can sing a godhead music. Deep-steel sky of snow and arch,
crimson robe and white

and blood: you touch the knife that's in your heart but still
you stand and ask for nothing, solemn by the stones.

I've seen this crownless king before. Approached a horse,
a hologram, another hum of silence
all around, vignette enclosed and spilling

soft-edged in the room. Berries in snow, fence way up
on foreign hill. Layers of time. The starved earth's rumblings.

Unwilling king, not king at all this tired teacher
dreaming of his censure when the gifts he gave
had all been spent and put away. Knows that wisdom

is an opening, a shifting snow-scene, trail down to the ocean.
Part of grace to sleep inside this place, ward of universe,

a constellation tuned inside. Trying different keys to slip
the opening, retrieve the blade and cauterize the cut.
To wear your pain myself. Hollow grail,

music of the hunt and shaft that takes to sky.
You and I have held each other's fingers at the end: you choke

and call for something from the edge to hasten it.
The unmoored wait with guarded eyes to sleep around you, hold your hem
as safeguard. Go no farther than the light will bear.

High Noon in Seville

Somewhere in the old town I walk towards your flat.
Occasionally my leather sandals slip on the century-worn
stones. Horses and their carriages are resting
under the sycamores. At this time of day even
tourists idle over their lunches. Chords
from a flamenco guitar bounce softly against
the tenement walls. There is that warm horse scent
of wood chips, dust, hay, and sweat. The coachmen
snore softly, committed to their siestas.

Your neighbor, the fat old woman, never looks up.
Her door is always open. The air is cooler in the hallway.
Temperatures in their forties C are only the beginning.
Summers are killers in Seville. The old woman smells
of animal buried in hot earth.
A smell so intimate I blush.

On this hot, lazy summer afternoon only the flies
buzz, the guitar stops and starts, a horse's
hoof occasionally clanks metal against stone.
I daren't ring your bell but knock.
Even the knocking jars.
Your sleepy face in the door frame,
lips pursed. There is a waft of summer sex
and perfume of an unknown brand.
Your skin can't lie.

Starting Over

Old and dusty, fusty.
The librarian in Babel.
First, letters drop from a turning wheel,
then words. Collecting all that's sacred
before the towers crumble. After all,
words carry the weight and mass
of extinguished suns.

The vulture allows the updraft to lift it,
finds dead languages and carries them
to its tome-lined nest.
But that is tomorrow.

Leather-bound books grow from ancient
burial grounds reaching for the light,
falling open on crumbling pages.

Parchments extol the virtue of silence.
When the quiet never ends
we know we are falling,
unencumbered by syntax.

Revert the wheel,
take back the words
to the beginning.

Don't Forget

don't forget the watermelon
you asked me to remind you &

though my conscious
memory has been filled in

by sandstorms & Morse code
I thought I should leave you this note

with its brief demands
for your time

how bright the sun
shines this afternoon

how warm the air &
scented like an oven baking bread

but don't forget the watermelon
pink in the meat like lipstick

sweet with juice
fastening your fingers to your lips

Women in the Suburbs, 1971

Mrs. Marsh with her tiny bouffant,
smoking Benson and Hedges,
the slenderest of all the cigarettes,
and eating pate on melba toast
with her husband, the dentist,
at cocktail hour in their study.

Not like my mom—a few doors away,
Squirting cheese whiz on a cracker,
her earrings made of little bird cages,
with tiny parrots swinging in them,
making me brush my teeth with baking soda,
making me pick up *dog dirt,* as she called it,
with a hand spade and a brown grocery bag
in the front yard.

Mrs. Lukernik, my best pal for a while,
the only adult who confided in me.
She gave me cigarettes,
made macaroni salad just the way I liked it,
and once observed that my mother was
a real *bitch* during menopause.
I heartily agreed, flicking my ash,
But I loved Mrs. Lukernik less after that.

Eventually I moved away,
packing the plastic stereo
with detachable speakers that Mrs. L
bought as a big surprise
and the pretty cotton dresses my mom
got from the Goodwill and hemmed.
*No one could possibly tell this came
from a thrift store,* she said to me.
Looking up, proud, pins in her mouth.

Visit

I NEVER LIKED my best friend's wife, Dee, not even when Jerry called me up and told me she was dying of cancer.

"She was diagnosed a while ago," he told me on the phone, "but now it looks like her days are numbered."

Dee never liked anything anyone ever tried to do for her. She was like Goldilocks. The bed is too soft, the soup is too hot. When the four of us got together, which we hadn't done very much since Jerry and Dee moved from New York up to Maine, Dee would bitch about the whole nine yards. From the car trip down, to the gas station ladies room, to our gravel walkway which she claimed hurt her ankles.

On the phone, Jerry said, "I want us to be able to see our best friends one last time."

"Great," my wife Peg said. "A love fest."

I expected Dee to be thin and gaunt, which she was. What I wasn't prepared for was her dying on our dining room floor. It was like the worst of all possible worlds. Jerry was Jerry, but Dee couldn't eat the pot roast because her teeth were bothering her. The twice-baked potatoes had too much garlic. Her neuropathy was kicking up and she claimed the glass of ice water I poured for her felt like a branding iron.

"Excuse me," she said halfway through the meal. "If I don't move my bowels right now, there's going to be hell to pay."

She got up, refused Jerry's offer to assist, made her way toward the bathroom, stopped, and then folded up like a plastic beach chair. Jerry was over her in a sec, raising her into a sitting position, telling anyone who would listen to call 911.

The paramedics were here is less time than it takes to tell about it. Two guys in their early thirties who made a good show of acting like the woman was still alive, when all of us knew she was roadkill.

At the hospital, the three of us sat around waiting until some guy stuck his head in and told Jerry to come with him. Once he was gone, Peg and I just starred at one another.

"Wow," I said.

"Wow is right," Peg said.

Some time went by before I said, "So what was for dessert?"

"Dates stuffed with goat cheese and blueberries," Peg told me.

She would have hated them, I thought to myself. But I kept it quiet. Instead I said, "What a weekend."

And Peg said, "Amen to that."

Crossing Over

Picking her way through milkweed,
the doe,

haggard, fur stretched
over her bones.

Then
hardly bigger than house cats,

twin fawns—leaping
to take her place.

G. F. BOYER

In Dad's Old Negatives

my ghostly brothers
pose in striped T-shirts,

awkward white-framed
spectacles. Arterial white

trees loom, a circulatory
system of memory.

At the kitchen table,
three kids, birthday, four

black candles.
Me, forking dark cake

into my mouth's fiery cave.

Silo and Barn

Blackened corn cobs floated
at the bottom. Last year's corn gone.
Now a scummed wash of rain.

You stuck your head
through a loading window
to look down.

Like a dark mushroom, its shadow
sprang into the square of light
sliding across black water.

—

All the long summer, you chewed oats
from the barn's wooden bins,
resigned and methodical as a cow.

Noise made cows give blood in their milk,
made chickens tuck a secret blossom
of blood into each egg.

Cracked,
that red and golden world
slid onto your plate.

JESSE BREITE

Cripple Creek

for Levon Helm

Down to Lake Charles, Louisiana,
he chased something bold as bonfire—
the golden luck of a careless woman—
good enough to holler about.

This too was my father's dream—
to be sent, to be mended and defended...
to live out that old
pig-in-the-python fondness for drunks,
to believe in shiny tickets at the race track,
to swear only by the odd myths
of hillbilly women, or not to say anything
when nothing is needed to be said.

I knew it first in junior high,
holding the disc, a shimmering highway
in my hand, and when I heard it,
I turned it up—the swelling beat,
the wobbling clavinet, the guitar's
curly stutter, the air-splitting voice.

And it ends with that vintage-pretty lie:
deep down I'm kinda tempted to go
and see my Bessie again
though anybody knows no matter
how deep that desire, he won't
go back—he won't even try.

Iridescence

for Ray Carver

At dawn, young light slicks the windows,
and the air is gentle as heartbeats.
The house is a hollow grey corridor.
My wife does hair and makeup,
and I make coffee. We both listen
for children, early in the summer streets.
We are always moving away from
what we know as enduring, collective.
The earth is fat and round, iridescent.
Who knew it was a dying pearl—that pearls
could even die? But we understand—
agree on the direction of the wind,
the colossal trees, the blood-thirsty trunks.
Nothing is as difficult as existing for more
than a moment—the endless exchange
of tongue and kiss, dollar bill and goodbye.
The clock throws its arms in circles.
How long until we realize it's trying
to hold on, to grasp the ceaseless spiral?
A blind man stands in the street out front.
I try to comprehend him, his aimless gaze,
but he doesn't speak a language I know.
A ways off, the highway cars spit water
and exhaust. The towers blink signs.
An expert knows the answers.

Spillway

Consider the drawers of water
rising with rain,
the way the lake swells
as shore reeds bristle gold
like the hair of a girl
fanned out
into the pull-tide of waves.
Consider the flood of a fine mist
that lifts off a moving body
of water.
Consider the dust orbs
that stream through a pale beam
of late noon light.
Consider what sinks and remains
bellied down
beneath that slit-brown
blanket of mud.
Consider the absolute dark
below, like a sheet pulled over
the face.
While above there is a search
party combing the shore.
There is a gathering
around the drain.

Apple Blossom Square Dance

Across the field of fork-raked furrows
in the gleaming furls of May moonlight
the dark pond of black soil reflected

I swam to the fragrance of apple blossoms
fleeing the women in white and green skirts
flowing to the fiddle, raising a fire

by tamping down desire with peg and sole hard to the floor.
Like white waterbirds the blossoms awaited,
eiderdown petals, plumage more silken than soft

perfumed forearms of women in flowering
white and green skirts flowing to the fiddle,
like eidolons of waterbirds the fluttering blossoms

as they fell. I remember the tow of those feathered waters,
my face enveloped in flowers and scents
searching for the firm shore of earth,

which the blossoms, like the mirage of women
in flowering white and green skirts,
moon-sprung and drifting, fragrantly denied.

A Round Straw Hat

I found a round straw hat turned upside down
on the wild grass of western Wyoming,
a great donation plate
with a pretty weave to catch coin
for the ravens resting there.

The hat does not wither and wilt in the rain
like an old fedora, the way in life
an old detective finds the past
has superseded the future.

It's not a cap,
pulled down to escape
the look of others, or to have
a look that others want to escape.

It doesn't speak of baseball,
bears no insignia of loyalty or brand
except the gift of toquilla
and the hands that wove it.

It's not a tam
or beret, a cover
for warmth. It's got a brim
to shed sunshine and rain, vents

in the weave to let my idle thoughts
vanish, then let them
find their way back
into circulation.

The Curse of Mao

ACROSS FROM THE Kashgar People's Park stands a statue of Mao Zedong. As tall as a building, with his back to Old Town, he is a symbol of the Chinese government itself. Always there, but with its back toward the Uyghurs. The young people ignore it, take their pictures in its shadow, but for an old woman like me, I see eyes that follow my movements and a hand that is raised, not in greeting, but before it strikes.

The young believe their protests, their talks with the government will work, that it won't, ultimately, come to war. Hope is the realm of the young. I have seen too many people die, too many disappear.

In 1969, the year the statue was first erected, I watched a young man and woman fall in love. His name was Yusef; hers was Mihrigul. I was already an old married lady then, preoccupied with my house and children, but I watched with everyone else as the courtship unfolded.

Yusef had graduated from University and was teaching philosophy at the Kashgar Teacher's College when he met Mihrigul. One of his students, she was equally smart and pretty. He was soon seen walking her to her dorm room after night class and visiting her at her parents' house on weekends.

Everyone in Old Town was happy for them. Mihrigul was a neighborhood favorite, with her ready smile and quick wit, and Yusef's family had been worried about his refusal to take a bride in an arranged marriage. It seemed their love came at just the right time.

When she became pregnant, her parents hastily arranged for them to be married. Seeing how in love they were, the neighborhood chose to look the other way, participate in the wedding without the usual whispers. We were prepared to watch them live a happy life.

They learned the child was due December 26, Mao's birthday. Normally, this wouldn't make any difference, but with the statue going up, standing exactly 12.26 meters high to honor the man, they laughed that even the Chinese government had blessed their baby. They took pictures in front of the statue and left love notes for each other in the space between its massive feet. Because of Yusef and Mihrigul, the statue stood for happiness. We watched them and we waited for the baby's arrival.

That was before Yusef saw a Uyghur man being beaten by a Chinese man in the street. He broke the fight up before the police got there, politely told them what happened, and wasn't surprised by the fact that he was arrested, too. No, the surprise came when he realized they weren't going to send him to trial, that he would be held as an enemy of the state.

One of the sympathetic Chinese guards helped Yusef get a note out to Mihrigul. She immediately went to the jail. It was hard for her, with her growing belly, to make the journey from Old Town, but Kashgar wasn't as big then as it is now. Every day, the police would let her in. Every day they were courteous. Every day, she had hope.

Until one day, Yusef simply wasn't there. They had no word on where he was taken or when he might be released. Even the Chinese guard who had been helpful had plenty of apologies, but no information. Yusef was an intellectual and therefore guilty as a matter of course.

Mihrigul took the situation with as much grace as anyone could have. She came home, cried, and went every day to the jail and asked the officials for news. She was so preoccupied with finding Yusef she didn't even notice when her baby stopped moving.

On December 26, they cut into her and found her baby had turned to stone. A "lithopedion," they called it. Mihrigul called it the Curse of Mao.

We never found out what happened to Yusef. Mihrigul left Kashgar soon after that, looking for her lost love. We never heard from her again.

On moon-bright nights in the town square, the statue of Mao looks as if it's lit from within. Tourists come then and take pictures with the glowing giant. If they are to fit the whole thing into the frame, the photographer has to stand way back, making the people look like smiling insects beneath the statue's feet.

Finding My Sea Legs

It's my first time fishing
        in forty years
the half-day boat nudging
        the pier's rosary
                        of bald tires.

Finding my sea legs
        I fish from the same spot
my father showed me
        as a child.
                        The boat anchors

close to shore
        the cliffs shrouded in fog
the tangled kelp rising rhythmically
        in the flat gray light,
                        home

to the white sea bass we seek.
        Unlike the anchovies of my youth
the bait is baby squid
        its manzanita red mantle
                        melts into my hand

while jetting between my fingers.
        Its enormous eye entrances
as black ink squirts into the sea.
        The skipper's laconic voice
                        soothing our lack of strikes
the bait boys eager
        gaffing a fish, untangling lines
tying a knot
        when I am unable to find my glasses.
                        The trek from the bait tank

a gauntlet of tackle, a deck slippery
    with entrails and silver scales.
Unsteadied by age
    my hand teems with life
                returning

to take my father's place.

Digging the Bog

*after the BBC documentary "Great Poets in Their
Own Words" segment on Seamus Heaney*

You wrote of your father digging
and I nodded along
as I considered

the purpose of the writer's life.
Then I heard you read
your poems,

saw you, in black and white
next to the peat bogs
where your father

worked, and I thought
of the bog bodies—
human cadavers

that have been mummified—
and wondered what
the bog does

to the unearthed potato: its skin
baked in soft earth,
its eyes on the edge

of sprout. I wondered
how much the mired
landscape shaped

the words that you dug
forth after living
where the dead

retain their skin and internal organs
yet find their bones
dissolved away.

I wondered what it does to any of us
when what we look like,
our facial panorama,

is so much of who we think we are
even as the writer inside us
craves the internal—

the "living roots"
that call us
to dig.

Wishbone

Shirtsleeves rolled
after church, my father
gouged his thumbs
through clabbering fat,
slid fingers under
roughened scrolls of skin,
the soft crack of bones
twisted to expose
what flesh remained,
and this placed safe
beneath cellophane.

Last, the wishbone
would come unhinged,
levered off, snapped
and set upon
the kitchen sill
to grow brittle
as its luck annealed.

Days later, the house
no longer warmed
by the smell
of grease and thyme,
the grayed tines
were taken
from their narrow
reliquary, and we'd
link our bones
in that votive yoke,
pulling in silent prayer
for the better share of grace.

ALAN CATLIN

Thoughts on Viewing the Fred Dana Marsh Painting, Chaos in the World 1918

1—

Death astride a black horse
hears the liturgical music of spheres
in the tolling of plague ship bells.
Holds the yellow flags of disease
the dead are wrapped in and offered
to rivers weighed down by the contagion
of bloating that yellow fevers cause
in the blood streams and the waterways,
the living drink from, seeking a palliative
to assuage the thirst of fever sores
and the heat of hydrophobic dreaming.

2—

The spinning globe is a world in chains,
the public burning, a systematic,
willful destruction of life like
the blank philatelic pages of a Central European
battlefield of unpronounceable names:
Bosnia, Herzegovina, Serbia, Croatia,
Montenegro, Slovakia, Dalmatia;
the seven sovereign republics of nowhere
overprinted by the white heated sword
of repression and of war.

3—

After the next war to end all wars,
the British Historian Hugh SetonWatson
observed that these lands were artificially
held together political units being fatted
for a violent revolution, a kind of anarchy
that would make the pogroms that preceded
the inevitable, ultimate political dissolution,
seem a tea party for diplomatic core wives;
a lesson to be learned from this, no?

4—

After the millennium, the pages are still
blank in the Central European album
where these countries are represented
by the oldest kind of overprinting,
the watermarking that comes
with the staining of blood.

The Secret

Everything in your life right now you attracted to yourself.

Thoughts become things.

You visualize a house, a Californian-style, sprawling thing of glass, brick and wood.
You are attracting this house to you. Visualize it.

You are living between these walls.

You do not have a fat husband who was once less fat, but now whose belly, hanging on
either side of his puckered belly button over his belt, makes you balk. You do not have
to deal with a fattie like him, not at all, and he doesn't force you to have sex with him
against your will just about every night. He does not smell.

There is no baby obsessed with nursing, forever hanging onto your long, stretched-out
teats. No, your nipples are firm and tiny, your boobs perky, not drained and deflated
from nursing two children.

You do not have a toddler from hell. He is not spreading peanut butter and jam
on the walls of your beautiful house. He is not adding crayon to the mix.

You are not on the phone with your boss, who is assigning you enough contracts
and paperwork to keep you up all night. She is not telling you to come in on Saturday
because there's a last minute meeting with those clients from China. Your job is not
on the line.

The baby does not have a fever. The toddler is not projectile-vomiting.

The fattie is not yelling at the children for crying. He is not hollering for more beer.
He does not leave a fattie-shaped dent in the sofa as he gets up to yell at you some more.

You are not holding a sharp knife over a sink. You are not thinking about the fattie's life
insurance policy.

You are not. You are not.

Blood

THE SOUND OF his wife's shriek from the backyard vibrated through the aluminum and plywood walls of the doublewide, across the floor, through the brown faux-leather of the La-Z-Boy, and up Jack Foster's spine, where it rattled his teeth and shook his brain loose from an afternoon airing of *The People's Court*. He turned the volume down and waited, frowning.

"JAAAAACK!"

He slammed his can of Milwaukee's Best, shallow and warm with backwash, onto the end table, an announcement to an empty trailer. He pulled himself from the chair with a grunt and a mumble. "Damn woman." Last he knew Annie Mae was hanging laundry. It was hard to tell what she needed.

Ever, really.

He heard the snarls and screams as soon as he opened the back door and started down the wooden steps. The stair structure, open, with a thin iron framework, rocked slightly as he descended. Annie Mae must have heard him.

"Get out here!" she yelled. "Peppy's got that damn groundhog!"

Halfway down the steps, Jack paused and thought about going back for his rifle. As he considered the idea, the boys emerged from the corner of his vision, running down from the woods. Earlier, Ned had burst in the front door asking for a hammer and nails. He and Dewey Burke from up the road were trying to build a fort out of sticks and logs. No way, Jack told him. The kid had no sense of what things cost. The notion prompted him to leave the gun behind. Ammo was way more expensive than nails.

Let the dog earn its keep. If he'd known how much it would cost to feed the thing he wouldn't have brought it home for Christmas, whatever year that was, three, four back. It seemed like a good idea at the time. A free gift for the kid. Now just a pain in the ass for Jack. It hadn't taken long, after he hurt his back and went on disability, to put the dog out for good. He wasn't put on this earth to cater to a dog that always expected something, accusing him with its eyes. The kid cried himself to sleep for weeks after that, and the fucking dog whined and howled.

Jack pushed through the line of hanging linen, where Annie Mae stood some five feet away from the clash of tooth and claw, urging the dog on.

The shed, like the trailer, sat elevated on concrete blocks for the times the creek flooded. The dog had the woodchuck by the back foot, trying to prevent it from getting under there, but that was like having a snake by the tail. The rodent kept twisting and biting as if it were made of something other than bone, bringing blood to the dog's hip and leg. Blood streamed from the groundhog's foot as well, but the appendage wasn't useless yet. The groundhog spun again, folding itself in half to open another wound in the dog's side with its vicious front teeth, staining another spot of the golden fur red. The dog yelped, jumped back, and then dove after the wounded foot again.

The boys stopped behind Jack, breathing hard, eyes wide. He glanced at them in time to see his son's anticipation turn to panic. No surprise there. As he'd figured out long ago, the eight-year-old was a pussy.

Annie screamed, "Get it, Peppy! Get it!" Dewey cheered with her and Jack laughed. Ned stood there, limp.

The woodchuck lunged for the shed again, but its foot was broken and the thrust was crooked. That was all the dog needed to get on top of the squirming animal and her mouth nearly vanished into the varmint's neck. Peppy had it now, pinned down, squeezing the air and blood out of the beast. It jerked wildly every ten seconds or so, and the dog clamped down harder, trying to shake it, a futile attempt to break its neck. Soon, the struggles came less frequently. The rodent's eyes went dead before its breathing, or the jerking, stopped.

The battle over, Jack's eyes fell to the boys. Dewey's expression was hard to judge, excited, but conflicted. His eyes kept moving between his best friend and the dead groundhog, his exhilaration retreating. Ned stood there, his mouth open, his eyes shedding silent tears like those weird-ass times when he was an infant, when the tears would just flow, his tiny mouth open but with no sound, and Jack would wonder if the kid had gone mute. Annie used to cry too when that happened. She said the baby could see his own fate, whatever the fuck that meant.

Well, there you go, he thought. This'll help make a man of him, show him how the world really is.

He turned back toward the trailer, taking one last look behind him. Annie was praising the bloody dog which was limping and Jack supposed she might be hurt pretty good. Peppy attempted to shake the dead groundhog like an oversized toy, but the carcass was too heavy and all the mutt could do was drag it around as she hobbled backwards in a circle, tossing her head back and forth.

Tears still coursed over the boy's reddened cheeks. Ned looked at his father, his eyes tightened into an accusation. It should have earned him a thrashing, that look, but Jack had better things to do today than whip an insolent kid. He turned his attention to the trailer, his mind set on another cold one and television justice.

Abebe

A BOY IN AFRICA has a distended stomach. Or rather, many boys in Africa have a distended stomach. This boy is named Abebe. He lies on a cot. His grandfather leans over the cot to stroke his grandson's hair back from his sweaty forehead. Abebe does not cry, nor can he talk. Breathing takes all of his energy. He wheezes like a hundred-year-old man. His skin is black but his face is pale, like old ashes. His eyes are as dry as sandpaper. His legs are weak and somewhat bowed. In fact, his thighs are barely able to support his body. There *are* tears in his grandfather's eyes, and his grandfather's tears course down his face. Various sores have infested the boy's skin. Some are bloody. The grandfather presses gauze onto the bleeders and the gauze sticks. Abebe gasps, choking on air. He is in a room with slow-moving ceiling fans and mosquito netting. The grandfather was able to arrange those things.

Abebe knows that most starving boys do not have cots, ceiling fans, netting, or even a grandfather. He is glad to have them but he doesn't believe they will help. Maybe it helps to have his grandfather here, but what can he do? Not much, Abebe thinks.

Abebe's grandfather knows full well that what he has accomplished is not sufficient unto the day but he can't tell that to Abebe.

Abebe's grandfather drove a taxi in Minnesota. He tried to get Abebe's parents to cross the ocean just as he had but they would not leave their home. They were murdered by rebels. Now there is no home. No home and no parents. Only his grandfather. Who is kind and worried but cannot save his grandson. Abebe is sure of this.

Abebe is ten, but he looks six. When he remembers his parents he wants to cry, though, as you know, he can't, not now. His father was a herder. His mother took in washing. Abebe had wanted a brother or a sister to play with but a doctor told her mother she could not have any more children.

Abebe's grandfather is holding Abebe's hand but he is afraid to squeeze it. He worries that he would break Abebe's finger bones if he did. When Abebe dies, it will the end of his line. There is no other child to carry on.

The ceiling fan sometimes stirs the netting and then the netting brushes Abebe's ashen face.

If only I had heard earlier! the grandfather thinks. He sends up quick prayers for his grandson—silently, because he doesn't want to alarm him.

Abebe wishes his grandfather could tell him how long this will last, this dying. He hurts. His chest, his stomach, his legs hurt.

Grandfather kisses Abebe's forehead and tells him he'll be back in a second.

Abebe watches the shadow the fan throws on the wall.

Grandfather returns with a doctor. "He will give you an injection to make you feel better, Abebe."

In Abebe's opinion, no injection ever makes anyone feel better. Needles hurt! But this sentence is too long for him to get it out.

The needle goes into his arm and of course it hurts. "You'll feel better soon," Grandfather says.

The doctor nods. "That's right, son," he says.

A tear appears in Abebe's eye. The right eye.

It stands there in his eye. It doesn't fall.

"Now, now," Grandfather says. "You'll feel better in just a minute."

And miraculously, Abebe thinks he feels a little better. The leg pains are easing, especially the pain at the top of his legs, where the buttocks begin. His various sores become less irritating. He stops thinking about them altogether. He can hardly believe it: the pain is being chased from his body. He thinks of the swimming hole where he and his friends hung out. He can almost smell his mother's cooking. He remembers the clapboard school he went to, and the nuns who taught him how to draw and read and multiply.

Grandfather is crying again. Abebe wants to tell him he can stop now. All the pain is going away.

MICHAEL CHIN

Watching the Dogs

ON THE SIDEWALK adjacent to Ocean Beach in San Diego, when the silver dollar sun turns a shade closer to copper, receding into a haze of fuchsia cloud formations, Gray holds Wilhelmina's sweaty hand and they walk atop matching pairs of flip flops, contorted to the shapes of their feet, with sand in every crevice.

A pair of tan-furred dogs run circles around each other. They race to arbitrary landmarks like a garbage can and a sewer grate and rub sides with one another. Their human trails a few steps behind them, red baseball cap, navy T-shirt stained with bleach spots, self-cut at the sleeves, unevenly—the left side at the seam so his whole shoulder is exposed, the other at a crooked angle so an inch of sleeve still stretched around his under arm like a pouty bottom lip.

And Gray imagines those dogs doubling back and choosing Gray and Wilhelmina over the man. Maybe they don't belong to him anyway. No leash. No tags. Maybe they'll ride back in the back of Gray's Impreza and stick their heads out opposite windows to let the wind peel back their ears and lap at the sky as it turned from salty ocean air to city engine fumes.

These two dogs curl around one another and sleep on the couch, and Wilhelmina wants to keep the bedroom door open far enough so the dogs can see them and know they aren't abandoned, but all the more so so that she can see them and know that she has not been abandoned. The next day Gray and Wilhelmina buy the dogs leashes and take them for walks.

The dogs adjust to a new apartment, with carpeting so they didn't scuff the hardwood when they chase each other or bound to the door when Gray gets home from work. These dogs learn not to play rough when Wilhelmina's belly and feet swell and she loses her balance. The dogs guard the babies and offer companionship come naptimes and serve as ponies for the children to ride their backs despite their mother's warnings they shouldn't.

These dogs keep Gray and Wilhelmina company after the kids move out. Older and grayer, they go for slower walks around the neighborhood streets and remember the beach and the sound of the ice cream truck that plays slowed down versions children's songs as though the recording could peter out at any second. And the dogs race at a slower clip to dandelions and after lizards, still making discoveries after all those years. Still wanting to do their humans proud. And Gray—he holds Wilhelmina's hand in an arthritic grip and remembers when the two of them were stronger and infinite and knew anyone not walking the beach at sunset was a sucker.

The man in the red baseball cap summons the dogs by name and motions. He and his dogs veer into the parking lot.

Wilhelmina squeezes Gray's hand. "What are you thinking about?"

Gray looks out to the ocean as an especially large wave crashes in the distance and the bobbing silhouette of a surfer rises and falls. Gray remembers that he is still young and not so finite and so very much in love. The smell of sand and suntan lotion fills him when he kisses her shoulder. "I was just watching the dogs."

DAVID CHORLTON

Five-Thirty A.M.

Before dawn, trains call out
as they pass through the city
while planes are scraping against low clouds
and sound from early traffic
overflows the freeway banks. Here comes
someone walking, someone strange
to our street, and he's striding out
with the purpose of a man who knows
where he's going and doesn't need light
to get there. He never stops to savor
the scent from citrus trees in bloom,
just moves as quickly as his feet
will let him, and he doesn't look quite
threatening enough to report,
which isn't to say he's welcome;
not at this time, when darkness
belongs to the cat who belongs
to nobody.

Out of the Weather

On a day darkening to rain
the usual discontent is palpable
on the streets, and the usual
complaints circulate so easily
they are not taken as a call
for change. It is the kind of day

that brings back memories
of days just like it, but far away
and years ago. There was no particular
reason to have been
in the silver grey town whose most famous
occupant had been dead a hundred years

and who lay behind glass
with her eyes waxed shut, her body
incorrupt inside
her sainted clothes, and rosary beads
resting slack around her wrists.
Visiting her may not have been

enough to have a non-believer reconsider
his position, but the suggestion
that miracles are possible
whispered from the candles
melting down. Night has fallen

with its traffic flow from red to green,
lights on the 24-hour stores
printed on the darkness,
and a few pedestrians out late
as if they had just

thrown their crutches away
and found somewhere to walk to.

Meditation Stroll

Stones define the path,
At first a spiral, then curving
Upon itself like the earth, a circle,
The universal prayer of stars and planets.

I am to walk cleaning my mind of notions,
Ideas, reverie, but the whisper of a poem dictates
Its small insistent rhymes
That I long to assemble. They too
Must be lost if I am to complete
This devotion. To unlock memory and then
Dispel it as one departs from a house
That will be demolished,
Taking nothing, leaving it all behind.

I am not adept at this. The hoofs of my
Imagination trotting a familiar road
As I try to follow this confusion,
This whirligig without ending like a poem
That offers no resolution.

This pattern is designed
For peace, I suppose. If I could cease
Thinking. Become the stillness of
A vessel emptied of water. I lack
A lack of impulsion.

Here is the lotus where Lord Krishna
Hovers in his bee-form. I should take no
Notice. But I buzz in the hive of myself.
Honeycomb. Sweet. Sweet.

Supper

HE ENTERS THE ROOM, throws them a look. Where two women are talking, he senses a conspiracy. And so he bangs drawers shut with a clatter of silverware, flings open the refrigerator, gulps milk from the carton, all in the outsized muscling way he has of inflicting his presence.

At the table, one woman is his wife, the other, his daughter. They are used to him and they continue talking while he paces from his den and back listening for clues. He thinks they changed the subject when he put his key in the door. If he accused them, they'd simply raise their eyebrows and look at him in imitation disbelief and he'd have to be insulted, maybe bluster off without his supper. So he says nothing. He victimizes the air willing himself to displace it violently. The women hate this, but they won't react. Each is aware of the small knot tightening behind the other's eyes.

"How was your day?" says his wife. His daughter flaps open the evening paper knowing he likes to see it first.

"Normal," he says, which means bad. A fine day would be extraordinary like winning money—like winning the *Reader's Digest* sweepstakes or the lottery. For years, he has printed his name on those cards, affixed stamps, sent them off. He buys the scratch-offs at the grocery store. Once he won. The most unlikely prospects are the ones he'll count on. The love of his family? Too easy.

The oldest girl, the one who no longer lives at home, was his favorite. He still thinks of her this way, although he never calls her or writes her a letter. That's how things get lost or broken, putting them into words and giving them away. When he recalls his elder daughter, how she would giggle when he hurled her in the air, how she gorged on mashed potatoes to please him, how she looked sleeping, blankets ajumble, he feels warm and good and that's enough for him.

His wife puts the plates on the table. She is a bad cook. Dinner is always a time of discord and disappointment. He unfolds the sports section. A good game on TV tonight. He thinks of this with pleasure. He'll have a beer, snack on cheese, the dog will sit next to him. If he feels like it, he'll pat her; if he doesn't, he won't.

JOAN COLBY

Shooting the Dam

JASON AND ZACH had been planning it all winter. Even longer, really, ever since autumn when the senior class took on the project of cleaning up Collins Island, a small protrusion of land that sat in the river just south of the dam.

Homeless people—bums, said Zach—camped out on the island, leaving it littered with beer cans, whiskey bottles, food wrappers and all sorts of unidentified trash. The kids filled dozens of garbage bags, raked the leaf-strewn paths, trimmed trees and shrubs, painted the wooden benches. They even partially repaired the rickety bridge that led from shore to the east side of the island. Some of the kids suggested it might be a good idea to tear down the bridge to restrict access. Nobody in charge agreed with that, so the winos and druggies soon returned with their backpacks, quarts of vodka and stolen grocery carts.

Jason had not been that tight with Zach before the island project. Jason was a good student, a quiet kid who took advanced placement courses in math. Zach ran with the jocks, a defensive back on the school football team. He had a herd of followers.

"You've gotta be bold," was one of Zach's sayings. And "better to die as a lion than live as a sheep."

Realistically, Jason didn't agree with that, but deep down inside it stirred something. He began to hang around Zach and his buds. "This kid's smart," Zach would say, clapping a hand on Jason's shoulder. "He'll end up a neuroscientist or something." More likely, a math teacher, Jason thought ruefully, but he was flattered.

That time on the island, looking at the swift flowing water coursing over the dam like a little Niagara gave them the idea.

"It'll be a cinch," Zach said. "Class of '05. Fixed Collins Island. Shot the dam."

All they awaited now was the spring melt to bring high fast-running water. Zach had a canoe and knew how to navigate.

"You just sit in the front and paddle," he told Jason. "I'll steer. You just do what I tell you."

Can't be difficult, Jason thought. They'd pick up speed, hit the dam, go airborne and sail on down the river. The plan was to land on the island. Their group of friends would be on the bridge above the dam watching.

"Are you guys for real?" Madison asked.

Jason nodded. "Why not?" said Zach, strutting a little. They planned to text everyone in advance. It would be like a flash-mob event.

April 15th was D-Day.

"A significant date," Zach said. They'd roped the canoe to the top of Zach's old Jeep and driven to the river. Both boys wore jeans, sneakers and parkas.

"You think we should have life jackets?" Jason asked.

"For what?" Zach scoffed. Their group would be recording the stunt with camera phones. "We don't want to look like nerds."

The day still held the chill of winter as they put the canoe in upriver at the Boy Scout landing. The river was high, lapping at its banks, white rivulets frosting its surface. Underneath, the current surged with a dark invisible force. Jason climbed into the canoe while Zach pushed off, then jumped into the rear and took up his paddle. They hardly needed to paddle though. The river seized the canoe and set it racing, so all they had to do was keep a straight course.

Jason laughed with excitement. "Wow!"

"Hold on. Hold on," shouted Zach as they flew downstream, aiming between the pilings that supported the bridge. At the lip of the dam the water roared in a white fury. "Go. Go," yelled their friends from above. The canoe went over the dam, but did not launch as the boys had expected. Instead, it plunged prow-first tumbling them into the boil, a foaming melee whirlpooling at the base of the dam.

Jason came to the surface, then submerged. Zach was nowhere to be seen. The crowd on the bridge screamed. In less than 15 minutes, the police were on the scene. Two divers suited up and went in struggling against the power of the river. Almost at once, they were caught in the boil, pulled down inexorably by the seething waters. The crowd screamed louder. The river roared in response. A group of cops running madly lowered ropes to their comrades. One seized the dangling loop, but the river tore it from his grasp and he disappeared, hauled downward into the hellish brew.

Everything was commotion, noise, panic. Cars pulled over, blocking the bridge and honking. People scrambled to the railing, hanging over and shouting. The wind picked up. Like a piece of flotsam, Jason was spit out of the boil, his padded arms flailing desperately as he was carried down to the island and washed up on the rocks, bruised and bleeding, but alive.

Three people died that afternoon. Zach and the two police divers, experienced men who knew the river. Their bodies were not recovered for weeks until the water receded and the river calmed, its rage satisfied.

There was talk of removing the dam, that dams like these were dangerous, had taken lives in the past. But nothing came of it. Over the years, some kid would shoot the dam again and live to brag of it. As for Jason, all he remembered was how the river held him and held him and then suddenly let go. As if it didn't want him. As if he wasn't worth it.

Tree

Its shadow on the snow
Is a crucified man
Or a hanged one. The images I conjure
Reveal a frame of mind
Designed by a brutal winter.
Days of ice. Days of sorrow.
The tree is blameless. Haven of the squirrels
Who dash along the fence boards
To seek something buried.
Like the pirates who can't recall
The emblems of the crumpled map.
Which of a hundred pines
Signifies the treasure
Guarded with a castaway's bones.
The tree has sucked its juices
Into its torso. Grey and old.
Branches broken like a promise
Of good fortune.
Behold the tree. Like everything: nameless
Until the serpent whispered a word
And the woman stared,
Her mind bursting like overripe fruit
That she tasted and relished
And shared.

The Jalals

streets winding like banyan vines
    a funeral procession coming through
the double doors of a temple

we drift into the poor village
    with its wooden slat walls
        and corrugated tin roofs
    rows of dilapidated huts
and women squatting in darkness

one man comes out
    from an alleyway shack
        with a butcher blade
and a bucket filled with blood

the river is choked with garbage

on Dewi Sita road
    children play
        in courtyard doorways
demons flare over garden walls

everything as intricate
    as the old school paintings
        Saraswati hovering in the forest
full of leaves becoming faces

Containing My Parents

Two rather small copperish cans
On top shelf of my bedroom closet
Remind me that my own somewhat living body
Ends up particled in a very small container
Stored wherever my children decide,
And that this so-important living corpse
I value as no other, may itself be
No more than something like dry rice cereal,
A grain I know a good deal
More about than I do about
My own assembled self.

I Think Her Name Was Maria, Actually

Sweaty teen greaser, wife-beater T,
unsnaps his jeans, plunges
between Tina's legs
or maybe Mary's,
over and over again,
sticky summer night, south Philly back seat
parking lot lights flicking off.

She thought it was love, I'm sure.

Nine months later, I'm born bastard naked,
unknown, unwanted, in shadows of Kennedy death,
corner hustler—yeah, some father—
out the back door.

I'm sure my birth mother's own father beat the shit out of her
before he sent her off to have me.
Good Sicilian girls don't fuck in the backseats of cars,
he probably said, as he took his belt buckle
to her pretty white skin,
but me, I guess, I'm glad one Sicilian girl did.

She was probably tall,
like me, with dark eyes, and a lot of dreams in her head.
I'm sure she was beautiful,
my ugliness a curse of my so-called father.
I hope she had a nice life without me

a life with birthday parties on Saturdays for her real kids,
a life with a husband who said he cared about her,
who gave her everything and told her he loved her
daily, like the paper in the yard, just inside their white picket fence

a sweet life where a judge's gavel doesn't echo in her head
the sound that makes her remember me

as suburbia swirls
in her head.

I think her name was Maria, actually.

GAYLE COMPTON

Hell Bound

Old Jackie's going to hell on the end of a poker

Singing on the praise team Sundays at
Abundant Tithings True Gospel Church of the Heaven Bound
in his fancy J. C. Penney's Levis
and testifying how he loves Jesus

Him with twenty-seven marijuana plants
growing amongst his corn and maters.

I'm talking ten-foot high,
pure gold leaf in-the bud female,
left-handed get-it-on catnip
and hash for cash.

He might be fooling them drones
and helicopters
flying over Doc Bill Branch
but he ain't fooling Jesus...
and he ain't fooling me.

I know my Bible and I know my—well,
I know what I'm talking about.

Frog Town Precinct

JUNEBUG CALHOUN had been on the election grounds since daylight. He was eighteen now and old enough to vote. Flathead Earl Adkins, the Square's inside man, was on hand at the schoolhouse polls to make sure the boy understood procedure, that he got his name on the big book and knew what lever to pull. Flathead could be quite an accom-modating man at election time, unselfishly lending a hand to anybody who had trouble reading or needed a little help in making up his mind. On a tip from Flathead, Junebug had already sold his Democrat vote twice: once to Eugene Pope for a dollar and again to Cabbage Johnson for a half pint of Early Times discreetly dispensed from the trunk of his '59 Nash Rambler. Afterwards, he drifted over to Granny's Grocery and Feed to see if anybody in the store wanted to buy him off with a Moon Pie and a can of that good cream with the picture of a cow on it. Junebug liked nothing better than standing in a room full of admirers drinking that sweet Carnation and explaining how the left per-sonality was always just slightly north of the right hypotenuse. And for five cents he would dance the Wild Turkey right there in the store, or maybe sing the chorus of "Simon Slick." These were just a few things he had picked up from Columbus Sowards to get girls. Not everybody understood it.

With a belly full of Granny's pasteurized milk and half a poke of Red Man in his jaw, Junebug stood on the railroad crossing with a hundred pound sack of chicken chop slung across his back, talking to Sonny Boy Harrison. He had been chewing and talking to Sonny Boy for a half hour, nearly, and not one time did he put down his sack. His chin, neck and belly glistened with sweat and amber.

As voting citizens of Frog Town, the two men shared their concerns about the Primary and the future of District 4. They talked about magisterial hopeful Jesus Leroy Pennington, a low-down bootlegger and Republican crossover they wouldn't trust in church with their granny. They lamented the whims and general decline of the local economy, the rooster fighting business in particular. Sonny Boy said Flathead Earl Adkins had crooked him, sure. He had traded Adkins two Roundheads and a 16-gauge shotgun for a little General, an easygoing bird that Flathead swore was the winningest rooster in three counties. "What I got," said Sonny, "was a chicken that wouldn't get his neck feathers up if you fed him carbide then blowed on his ass."

They talked about Square Robinson, the incumbent, and what a lying sonuvabitch he was. Sonny said old Square had been putting off giving him a job with the county for four years now, knowing he could run the piss out of a John Deere backhoe. Junebug said he felt the same way about politics his old man Minus did. No registered voter should ever have to leave his house and go all the way down to the Square's office at the end of the month to pick up his commodities. Nosiree! Every law abiding citizen had a right to his government relief, to his cheese, powdered milk and butterbeans. They ought to be delivered straight to a man's door, and the Square ought to have to do it.

"This is America, by God!"

Citizen Lobster

a.k.a. Lobster Thermidor

Surface cool, its strict, glass green
geometry bespeaks
a world that is too perfect,
whose elect seem oblivious
to the fog of algae that stains
the once pure waters. A steady
stream of admirers passes by.
Someone waves a taped claw.
After clandestine meetings
in a far corner, a delegate
is sent whose transformation
brings a hush to the world beyond.
In murmured appreciation,
guests talk of a certain Cafe.
Few remark on the play, fewer

the month, none the day. The chef
is Russian. Each dawn, the dazed
converts huddle close in what is
their last collective act.
They are surrounded by clouds
of fingerprints that last
till a spray bottle's quick rain
clears things up. Their watery docket
tries even their patience. They do not
know their verdict had been
rendered long ago. The sentence
involves mustard, brandy, eggs,
a cheese crust, and a change to some
headless other, shell split
and dished on bone china.

J. L. COOPER

In Case of Rapture

LIMPING FROM A TURN of an ankle, I stumbled to a park bench before the advent of a swollen sea. The bench was carved by messages of hate, gouged and memorialized in pressure-treated fir. Declarations of faith were just as deeply made, so I couldn't tell who was more in need—haters, or believers.

Pain brought me to the grain in wood. I came face-to-face with a carving of a delicate feather and a small letter *V*. A scar you might say, if it wasn't so beautiful. A shuffling homeless woman claimed the other end of the bench, with a lunchbox in her lap. I was a brittle, sorry version of me, but she broke our silence, saying, "The *V* is me. How do you like the feather I carved?"

I said I loved the image, that she had a gift for sure. I was thinking of the bird's-eye view of the little park, with so much grief below, where most have nowhere else to go. I was looking at garbage everywhere, but *V* dismissed my glance, saying a single feather should be enough to make anyone pause and wonder, if they have any pause and wonder left in them.

She looks for feathers in mornings. She said possessions get in her way. When she finds a feather suitable for permanence, the whole world comes in view and she begins her solemn work on knees too old to feel. People can use the bench when she's finished. *V* puts the feathers back to where she found them. In case of rapture, she doesn't want to be the one to alter what has fallen. "That's my life. I guess you could say I'm patient."

V didn't ask for food or money. She asked about my pain. She spent last night on a hard plastic chair in an ER just to get out of the cold, then carved the feather in our bench with the tip of a broken can opener. I was the first to see.

V took me to nearby benches to see her other carvings: she with a shuffle, I with a limp. She said I could steady myself on her shoulder, but I didn't want to add my burden to hers. Don't bother asking her story. I tried. She thought she heard a peregrine falcon overhead, then gathered her breath to make it to a bench beyond a sycamore, and asked me to leave her there.

"You are very kind," I said.

"You have a smiling sadness," she replied.

I've returned to thank her several times, and offer art supplies, hoping not to offend. Pain can make visions appear—and there is dignity to ponder. I haven't found her yet, and hope she's safe from cold. I walk her trail of feathers, imaging the wood that knows her careful hand.

Jiggety-Jig

They say you can't go home again,
so I did.

Two decades' drought made my childhood
home hard as a sponge dried of memory.

When I was eight, Grandpa
gave me that anatomy book and said,
"Boy, don't ever get in the habit
of seeing people as smiling skeletons
just because you know what's under the lid."
But teeth were just bones after that,
and eyes just sockets to the soul.

So with the house. Mere skeletal
parts now: Concrete dandruff
under front step risers, squinting
windows, a show of moss stubble
on the shingles.

There's the rusting oil pipe near the back
wall, at least, calling
"wait a minute" real friendly-like.
"Don't ever let me see you sniffing
that again," Mama once warned.
And I didn't. Till now.
No cars in the driveway, so what
the hell. I steal over, twist the metal cap,
deep-toke 80-proof vapors of heating oil.
Sweet Jesus, I think, taking more drags.
Real as a rib!

The corner garden?
A garden of gone now.
All those hours and days as a juvenile
inmate pulling weeds by the hair,
shaking dirt from the legs.

I give the back door
the look—the one reserved
for folks who cultivate dandelion,
chicory, and clover from fake
leather La-Z-Boys.

"Can I help you with something, sir?"

Jesus, but I jump. A man. Framed
by my old bedroom window yet.
I'm disoriented. Heating-oil haze,
maybe. Looks like Dad blurred by screen
storm. Or Father Kelly's shadow-whispers
at the dark grille of the confessional
in Sacred Heart.

"I used to live in this house," I smile
with all the confidence of the condemned.

"That's nice," he says. "But maybe you should
be going now instead of standing
in other people's backyards."

Other people. So *they're* the ones. Saying
you can't go home again, I mean.

I hate being kicked in the ass
by a platitude.

The Lotus Eaters

"WE'LL GET ODD being alone so much in the middle of nowhere," my wife intoned as only a native of Intone Nation can.

"What," I said. "Who wants to visit this old camp anyway? Back on the highway, the sign says 'Maine, The Way Life Should Be,' but here it's the way life 'used to be' and nobody wants 'used to be' anymore. It's used. Like cars before they became pre-owned."

"It's beautiful here. It should be shared with company," she countered with her deft wifely deafness. "Our friends would love the lake, the woods, the loons. Who can resist loons?"

"*Your* friends, not ours. Will you stop with the language games already?"

So it was decided in a 1-0 vote: Her friends from Boston would visit on Fourth of July week. The next morning, I found a list on the kitchen counter. I wove new wicker seats for the canoe. I stained the floating dock for sunbathers. I sanded and painted the old Adirondack chairs to stare at the summery stars riding the milky river.

And it seemed at first my wife was right. Her friend Debbie said, "Oh, it's darling!" Her friend's husband, Frank, said in his manly, arm's-length way, "Nice place you got here. Is there a basement?"

"The water is pumped off the lake," I said, "so don't drink it when you brush your teeth. And there's a cesspool—grandfathered—instead of a septic, so keep your showers short."

As if I was giving off a skunk-cabbage odor of my own, my wife guided them away for a tour of two bedrooms—brief, but long enough for me to stop talking grandfathers and cesspools.

Later, we drank because that's what guests do. Frank settled for Geary's Ale because I had no Chivas Regal. Debbie settled for Australian chardonnay because I had no Grey Goose.

About a half hour into drinks, Frank shifted and dug into his pocket. "What's the password here?" Casual. Like he'd asked how often it rains or the median temperature for July.

Debbie smiled at me. "We know," she said, "that Katherine works here so you can be together. It's so darling you have cable and internet in a place like this."

"Just like Thoreau," I smiled.

"It is thorough for such a rustic setting," Debbie replied as Katherine gave over the password. Frank entered it and Debbie said, "Wait!" and fished her smart phone from the dark pool of her purse.

The talismans did not return to pocket and pocketbook for the duration of their visit but took places of honor like shiny attendants beside them.

We talked some more. Debbie's phone chimed. She looked at its black mirror, mirror and smiled, the fairest of all. Her thumbs danced its cuneiform keyboard and she carried on the conversation. Like nothing had happened.

Later, Frank's phone burst out in song. "Born To Run." The Boss picked up immediately. He talked into the balsamed Maine air too loudly, as if his phone were elderly or a foreigner.

At dinner he pointed his device at the Geary's bottle on the table to find out what the other, ether world thought. "There's an app for that," he explained.

When I took him out on the dock at 11 to introduce Vega, Deneb, and Altair, he pointed his device at Scorpio and, like the Learned Astronomer, announced, "Ah. Antares."

There's an app for that, too.

Our guests demurred on canoeing when the lake woke in its glistening, morning mood. They did not comment on the loon's lonely call. Or the scratch of the nuthatch as it fussily circled the great white pine outside our kitchen door. Or the watery song of the wood thrush high in the birch.

They did not swim. Or walk in the wood. Or fish off the dock. They stayed inside, mostly, heads bowed, monks praying over pocket breviaries, sleepy-eyed communicants calling on their Wireless God gazing down from St. Peter's satellite.

Yes. God. There's an app for that.

On the third day, Debbie asked the town's name again so she could search stores. Tapping and stroking her device, she wrinkled her nose. "What about Freeport. Are we far from Freeport?"

Frank said, "L.L. Bean's anchor store is in Freeport," as if this was breaking news.

We left lake and loon behind and drove to Freeport. The day after, it was Kittery to the south.

"How far are we from the outlets of Conway?" Debbie hazarded the afternoon we returned from Kittery.

"Too far," I replied, because my wife was out of the room and I could.

The next morning our company finally left. A day earlier than planned.

As soon as their Lexus rolled out of sight on the pine-needled, dirt road, the camp grew morose and silent and resentful.

I turned to my wife: "Hey. At least we're not getting odd."

3:30

In the dark
from over the water, a rooster
celebrates my insomnia

At the Moulin Pastelier

That night in the Lauragais, we sat on the lawn swing
watching the moon's bright sickle slice the deepening
sky, the long spill of landscape flushed with sunset.
From the woods, we heard two *hiboux*: "*Qui vous? Qui vous?*"
The bands of color faded, smudged into each other like chalk
pastels. This auberge was a *pastelier,* an old mill for turning
woad into blue dye. Here, they dried the plants, ground them
to paste, let it ferment, then molded it into *cocagne,* balls
the size of grapefruit, let them sit for six months. This
was the famed Land of Cockaigne, where all you had to do
was lie on your back and watch your wealth dry in the sun.
How to get rich in the 16th century. And how sweet
this evening has turned, hearing the owls, the only birds
that can see the color blue. Gauguin said *if you see
a tree as blue, make it blue.* Our room here is painted
pale duck egg. *The devil* said Mitch Ryder *has a blue
dress on.* I say the night is equal parts hydrangeas
and sapphires. You say *honey, it's getting cold.*

BARBARA CROOKER

On Reading Charles Wright on a Fall Afternoon,

sitting in an Adirondack chair, paint peeled mostly off, just the pentimento
of green.... Not a cloud anywhere; the pure blue verb of the sky.
The sun slants down, limitless, even as I'm feeling my days,
and how they are numbered, wondering how many more autumns
I've got in the bank, how many words are left in the pen....
In this post-modern world we are not supposed to talk of the presence
of God, but I know after surgery, someone came into the room,
invisible, and held my hand. No birds are singing or flitting from bush to tree;
even the lawn seems to have given up, exhausted, exhaled its last green breath.
The dead come back, but they no longer speak our language. Ring me like a bell
in this brassy sunlight; wash me clean. Speak in the tongues of flowers.
The kudzu is covering the trees; they bend, but do not break.

DEDE CUMMINGS

Lament of the Glaciers

"...for not even the flutter of a fly's wing is as fast as change."
—Simonides of Ceos

I pray to the final human being
on earth, the last one standing,
on the edge of what once was
thick blue gray ice the size
of Manhattan. She is not
wrapped in fur, but laced
with claw marks from ivory talons;
she squints through cataracts,
tormented by what remains
of what was once a frozen sea,
to find a precipice; she
drops to all fours, looks around,
and panting from the effort,
throws a stone in the direction
of the wind.

JIM DANIELS

Miracles

I'm sorry for praying to God
    to bring a snow plow down my street.
He knows and I know that I'm not one of His guys,
    but the mayor's Hot Line is wailing busy as a siren.
I even confessed to mother-fucking the neighbor on crutches
    who accused me of shoveling snow on his car.
When we got the first two feet, people were taking photos
    of beautiful drifts. Then tree branches
cracked off, power lines down. Then we had to shovel.
    Then car after car, stuck, abandoned at odd, mad angles
of the possessed and despondent. My age, 53, started
    speaking up: back, shoulder, elbow,
etc. After the third foot, craven altars to false gods
    arose clumped on street corners.
Weather people erupted in flamboyant orgasms on TV.
    They train people on the hot lines to be patient and nice.
    I think they kidnap old grandmothers
and feed them candy lipstick. This morning
    I woke to the blessed rumble of the plows
gathered on the corner. I ran out and waved them down,
    dancing on mountains of snow. I would say
as God is my witness, but I'm not so sure He's still around.
I left an apologetic note on the crutch guy's windshield
    and searched for my own car buried blocks away
where I abandoned it after drunk college students refused
    to help. Sainthood is a long, drawn-out process,
like the death penalty. One guy's miracle is another guy's last meal.
    It's snowing again, or still. They are laying hands on
the giant green screen map on TV, evangelists
    for disaster. The snowplows scrape away six days of it.
Will I see another storm like this in my lifetime?
    I trudge out into it—in my lifetime, in my lifetime,
in my lifetime—too deep to make an angel
    without disappearing.

Fragrance

The catfish freed of my hook is thick
with angry twitching whiskers
until I hit it with a hammer.

Cosmos of roe in the mud at the tip of a flea
market folding knife, armed with leather
punch & de-scaler. I use neither.

Other earths have many moons, mine
is selfish by nature. It's a learned thing
to insert the knife & slice up to the jaw.

I was a caesarian baby, my big head
stuck in a hip-cavity. My mother flips
catfish steaks on the grill, wafting epiphany.

Desert Skull

In the skull is the cathedral
    for the unlettered and the lame.
      Sunlight delivers sermons through each eye socket,
    wind shimmers like an unfinished homily
and sands berm up on each ear
    perfect angels with wings about to break
      into white and fly.

So what if the skull isn't a man
    or a woman, could've been a man
      or a woman with darkness and constellations
    inside the fists massaging landscapes of skin,
rearranging sins, clearing for meditation.

Inside a desert or outside a desert
    there is no need for the perfect priest
      or mullah or rabbi
        no need for tribal wars, no need
    for guns, just hands massaging skin,
bodies singing the most human song

which is the song of thanks
    the language of saints in fountainheads
      water pouring over and over.

JOHN DAVIS JR.

Grief Yard Work

His lawn is never neater than when he mourns:
Chopping hawthorns into spheres of denial,
he decimates flowerbed weeds with hoe-blade and ire.
Death in the family means bringing blunt ends
to overgrowth, to softness—wood and leather,
sweat and blisters make salty pain paths, placating rage.
He cuts no bargains, but grass and brush
are laid down into green pastures and valleys.
By day-labor's finish, his burn barrel saddens
with ashes. Grey remnants' simmer turns him inside
toward supper, a communion akin to acceptance.

Steam Shadows

In this city summer of longer light and higher heat,
they're there—trembling, near-transparent signals
cast by sun and moisture, waved onto weed-broken sidewalks
and faulted asphalt continents adrift: our basketball courts.

Almost as invisible as shorter words, slicker skins
this season brings, their slight shade is just different enough
like our nets that aren't really nets but rusted chains hanging
from once-orange goals weathered into sharp-crackled, flaking brown.

North side boys hear sweet swishes when they shoot—
cotton's kept white year-round inside the air-conditioned Y.
They don't dodge holes, dip-slip around pea-gravel patches
or stop short of a dunk to avoid finger cuts and missed games.

Their voices echo back to them; ours keep going into the streets.
We grow knowing sweat, knowing dark, knowing beyond
won't stop the sound of our work-play, our possibility.
We are steam shadows. Look here: we are rising.

To Former Neighbors Who Moved to the City

Concealed by tall buildings, sunrise and sunset
no longer hold sway in your blockaded lives.
PM is AM is FM and all matter is beige:
cubicles, bathroom stalls, your uniform house
approved by the HOA—*acceptably neutral.*

It is winter here, and our Bahia has faded
to a light brown, but its green will return
by spring. Our children will hunt eggs
with new kids on the circle who've come
from a landlocked square state out west.

Their parents have painted the door once yours—
it is blue and colonial, contrasting red brick.
Morning and evening spread their frequencies
through our oaks, speckling our yards
with warm white pixels like skyscraper windows.

Admiral Onishi's Amends

HE MUST HAVE KNOWN. Alone. Past midnight. Black, oily blood. Somehow, he must have known. It wasn't enough. He did it anyway.

He was drunk. That was part of it. And the war had ended. And though it had been obvious for some time that it would end the way it did, still, he hadn't expected it. He hadn't thought he would live to see it. He was the type of man who people always said wouldn't make it to war's end.

The sword was heavy, and the flesh tough, but what surprised him the most was the weight of his intestines sliding onto his lap—a black, steaming mass in the middle of his clean, sparse bedroom—when he raised himself into a crouch so that he could push his neck onto the blade. But after he pulled it out of his stomach he found he couldn't do it. He was too weary. The shock was too quick. And he knew, despite everything, that it wasn't enough. To end it there wouldn't be enough.

Four thousand pilots. That was the number on his mind. It was a small number in a war where a hundred thousand could die in a single night. But still, it was a special number. Four thousand dead, and he had killed them. He had as good as outright killed them. They were his pilots, his kids, and he had promised them so many things. Whatever else he did, it wouldn't be enough. Not anymore. Even now, losing blood, barely conscious, he must have been aware of it.

Midnight turned to dawn, and dawn turned to bright, hot morning. He couldn't believe it. Blood still pumping out, even after all this time. Fresh blood onto old. Slick red onto matted brown. And when he was discovered around noon, and he was conscious, he still couldn't believe it. The roar of cicadas when the man opened the door. The smell of midsummer. That baked, bitter smell.

The man called a friend, and the friend called a doctor. After that, more friends. They gathered around him. They spoke in turn. They told him that he had done enough. Of course he had. It was all he could do. The racking pain. The interminable wait. He alone had done what so many others had promised. He had paid his debt. Atoned for his sins. Followed his soldiers to the place where he had sent them. Some said this in soft, gentle tones. Some laughed it, or barked it, as if it were obvious. Some only nodded it, or cried.

He died at six. The sun turned brown as it slipped toward the trees. The screen against the windows glowed. His friends were still there, one forgotten palm on his shoulder, one absent stare at his chin. Fifteen hours. Someone told him that. It was a long death. But it was a short amends. Too short, of course. He knew.

WILLIAM DERGE

A Calendar of Simple Pleasures

Like that old *abuelita*
at Magruder's supermarket
picking through the mangoes,
I would like to choose my days,
Sunday mornings, for instance,
fresh and almost too sweet,
or Friday evenings,
when the groaning stem gives out,
and you have to eat your freedom fast.
I would like to be able to
squeeze the hours,
to check their ripeness,
or ask for a sample slice
of a June afternoon,
reject the bruised items,
or steal a grape from a cluster
of weekends.
I would fill my cart
with the passion fruit of a new affair,
or persimmons of a seasoned love.
My calendar would be
a select bin of desires
where nothing ever rots
or goes bad
or attracts a single fly.

LYNN DETURK

In the Anglican Cemetery

St. John's, Newfoundland

Even high on this hillside there clings a morning mist
that holds me close as drawn breath and whispered words
that wets my face and lashes slides its fingers down my neck
until I am chilled as the North Atlantic
when icebergs sail south from Labrador

I walk in this place read history here
touch it with cold fingers as they trail along
the gray silhouettes   Crosbie   Baird   Barrett   Chaffe
an archive of historical consequence writ in stone
merchants and ships captains tinkers and fishermen
every one of them reeking of cod

forsythia weeps over the path blossoms spent
a foghorn's mournful note floats up from the harbor
lingers then dies leaving a vacancy filled
by the hushed tread of my feet on the pebbled walk
I search and finally find him my missing friend
so recently birthed into this raw earth
the sign of his passing a dark loamy scar

all those around him are clearly labeled
yet his place is marked only by a crystal glass
filled with rum and left instead of a headstone
a Papist's tradition for waking the dead
and to me for whom such things are no matter
I marvel Peter squeezed through those wrought iron gates
the founding fathers placed to keep the Irish out

LYNN DETURK

Tors Cove, Newfoundland

...is a long way from St. Louis, Missouri

She is dying   3000 miles   four time zones away
Don't come   I am told   *There's nothing you can do*

and this truth is irrefutable   it marks a stark acceptance
and triggers irrevocable regret when I don't go

for I don't know if anyone strokes her cheek   her forearm
whispers into her ear   clasps her hand palm to palm

in life's last handshake   making that raw
primal connection available only with the dying

or do they sit back from the bedside accompanied by the sound
of turning pages as she sleeps those last few hours away?

I pace the rocks at the continent's edge   prowl spaces
where waves come ashore   stare out to sea   searching the horizon

for what lies beyond   and I hear her in a thousand iterations
say the last words we ever shared   *When are you coming to see me?*

103

Puzzle Dust

MY FRIEND'S PARENTS went sailing for an entire summer, leaving him in a cottage on Georgian Bay with his grandpa and three Labrador Retrievers that never stopped barking.

"Don't they keep you up at night?" I asked, seeing the dark circles beneath his eyes.

"My walls are pretty thick," he said. He mumbled something else. His lips were thin and puckered. Everything else about him looked tired.

"They kill animals and bring them to my door. Last week they killed a fox," he said, digging through his grandpa's sock drawer to find rolling papers. At fifteen, my friend already had a developed taste for the finer things. He kissed a joint together with the precision of a veteran stoner.

"Where are your mom and dad now?" I asked. Both our parents kept boats floating offshore of the posh Windermere Marina. We had a mutual aversion to the sea.

"Atherton, California," he declared, in a flippant, highfalutin' voice.

When I slept over we searched for games, sneaking into the kitchen for munchies whenever the dogs went outside. We went through every cupboard before finding an unlabeled box underneath the sink, obscured by a sheet of dirt. I hoped we would find one of his grandpa's guns, or an extravagant marijuana pipe. Instead there was a mismatched jigsaw puzzle. I grinned at it, realizing we now had a summer project, split into a thousand tiles.

One afternoon, when nearly five-hundred pieces were fully interlocked, my friend said I was smarter than him. I didn't know what to say, because he wasn't necessarily wrong. I had constructed most of the panoramic landscape by myself while he got high and read comic books or dirty magazines.

"What do you want to be when you grow up?" he asked.

"An archaeologist, but I'm not totally sure."

He took a quick drag, then looked at me with eyes that were stale and dim.

"My parents are never coming back," he said.

He explained that his parents were moving to the States and that he was to stay in Canada. That way he wouldn't have to get used to living somewhere new halfway through secondary school. They wouldn't live together as a family, but they would send him letters.

The week before summer ended we finished the puzzle—a beautiful portrait of the Valley of the Ten Peaks. Tracing my hand across Moraine Lake, I revered its dazzling blue. There was one empty space at the crest of Mount Little. I gave the tile to my friend. He took my hand and we pressed the piece down together. Then I saw it in his face. He was already a man.

Twenty-Year Vows

I.

I gave you Chinese food, vegetables, enchiladas.
I gave you a place to be: watching me practice

my high school play, making out
in a dark car, wherever you could be

but church or college. Now I give you a brand new
Tuesday, never redone. I give you a ride to Sonic

when you're drunk. I give you a place to complain
about work and space to keep working. I smash your

habits when they spin like the washer. I give you wild
books and plot twists. I break your routine

splintered like glass. I break your life so it can never
look the same again, so I'm fused to your bones.

II.

You give me eggs and bacon every day. You give me
chili gravy, chocolate covered Oreos and Southern Comfort

peanuts on Mother's Day. You give me an alarm
a daily wake-up, a one-more-warning.

You give me a place to be nothing and left alone
like something exceptional.

You give me a place to be worthless and covered
in blankets and pillows. You give me

a pocket to be kept in or let go. You give me a buoy
to return to, an ocean to sink through,

a lifejacket that looks like
a weight.

Gravity

A hundred hushpuppies, Wildman beamed, *don't doubt the vacuum.*
Shotgunned beer sealing the brag, he bellied up to the tailpipe
of virtue, huffing cornmeal moons past crag-and-crater chompers.
Jabbed to his glottis in shop class, that black hole sucked crumblies
big-banged in Silver's snare drum batter and defibrillator splash.
Near a gentleman's D, Wildman's cheeks pearled like implants
he couldn't swing, and his pirate eyed the plank—
a pickup dotted with Plutos of rust, blinding sheet metal and beer can—
along which Wildman twinkle-toed, bombing with a slurry of Coors,
golden sludge, and rings of Pepto his acid tag. Then the spongy clavicle
of afternoon shrugged into dusk, and he blazed tonsil aura on his fender.
We knew it'd come to this, Wrong Way signs half-seen, our launchpad
drooling *I done had my fill boys.* But Wild cottoned Long John's mojo,
riding fryers and skirting fallout through the acne grease of high school,
so when he peeped the potion, toking backfire brigades of testosterone,
he downed a shot of malt vinegar, hitching his star to a spidered windshield.
Sometimes you want to wrap a man in cloud and hurl him into the blue.

The Rope Swing

after Melissa Range's "The Rope"

You used me. To taunt and tease, to lure the ripe
and lithe, the slurring and show-me, the no shirt,

no shoes, no service crowd, the limber with sixers
of swill, the brought-low lugging coolers of snarl.

That's the thing, to hang I'll sway in any neck
of woods; to swing I need a hole deep and wide.

No boys in blue, nervous nellies, moms and dads.
I'd like an elm or maple, though an oak will do.

You looped and tied me, made of me a ring around
a giant's finger, barky and brown, strong as bone.

Still I've snagged an oldster's shoulder blade, the gray
blazing his brow enough to make me quake, squall.

Yes, I've concussed, I've busted knees, I've split arms
in two, like kindling from my fingernails. The last

chortle a sec after Davey Long's final breath,
that was mine. I watch over years sentimental,

warm, past. Beware, the New River's anything but,
my fray a flotsam of vinegar and piss, skin, musk.

To ride me, fathom the depths and check the knots.
Get your head right, mainly. Then, leap, let go, pray.

As I dreamed, you let me let the children swing.
Mind your wants. I got my wish and still I killed.

PHILLIP T. EGELSTON

Anniversary

for Bryce Berkowitz

Amber-light ripples lathered
the dock where, fresh from our
confluence, you always looked
like the rouge of a fine sunset.
All the old ice of winter had
melted, warming our lips, the
lips of snow. Didn't we kiss
until all the valleys sang green?
Our hues were those of such
cajun skies that we smoked
under ermine eaves of fur. I
was your nose-studded boy
riding the roads of cedar—
striped in a red and white tank-
top. Wasn't I *zazzed* and on
high? Wasn't I the one
priceless as gin and juniper?

What years we had, without a
clock or a watch or anything
like *security!* And now we have
flown over so many deltas'
waters, to meet this pleasant moon's
soft light that allows me to know you
shoulder-high and tallied beyond
my sleekest dreams—sneaking
into the bathroom at night,
while I still lie on the rumpled dock
where I never forget to
melt into all the ways you
always get it right. Was there
ever a time we ever knew
there *wasn't* another year in us?

Trying to Call Forth a Ghost

When I want to feel regret,
I pull out house keys that you left me,

circle our old neighborhood,
cut across the alley, near Reese Park,

where we claimed swings like kids,
and pumped our legs to reach the sky.

Then, I drive down Landon,
pull in front of the house, contemplate

exiting the car, walking to the porch,
turning the knob.

Each time, I never do it,
but imagine that one day

the figure approaching the porch will be me,
and the cats will greet me, while you pause

your painting or grading to ask why
my return took so long.

A Real Sweet Thing

AFTER MY FATHER DIES, I'll have to find someone to buy the bears. His dying is taking longer than expected—the white-sheeted bed the hospital set up for us in the sunroom is actually brightening over the months.

"Don't go too low on the saddles," he tells me one day. "Those'll sell for a lot, don't let them talk you down." The saddles are extra large—true—thick and leathery. He spent a fortune on them, but who will buy them now? What horse's back can they fit? I don't tell him this. I'm not worried about the saddles.

There is so much dead grass. I peck at my nails in the window every morning, watching the furry thistle of bear hair slowly accumulating against the back of the house. Bear hair, horse hair, an overwhelming amount of cat hair. It takes me a long time to get to know the father who bought the bears.

"Will the walls hold?" I ask him. I imagine horse carcasses in all of these conversations—thick red stripes of clawed bellies.

"Sure."

Six months earlier, he bought loads of electric fence, round pens, built thin concrete walls. He is looking out on the pasture.

"Do me a favor," he says. "The big one—the girl—she's been warming up to me; a real sweet thing she'll turn out to be."

I will not train the bears, like I know he will ask. I will not try to ride them. There has only been one day, I've learned from him, that he was able to measure the saddles against one of the bear's backs—the one named Simon, the big, orangey-black one by the back fence.

"Fantastic," he tells me, about the way he got the bear near the fence, how he reached his hand through the metal bars. "There's nothing like a bear six inches from you to make you remember why you do this." The saddles are sloped to fit their backs better, and he tells me he can climb on them once the bears are more settled.

"And then what do you plan to do?" I ask him. Do I remind him that he is dying? Everything is future tense. "A bear-riding farm?" I almost laugh. No one will come, I want to say. "Rodeos? Circuses?"

"Why do I need to show them off?" he asks me. And I can see it: my father coming around the side of the big blue house, his legs draped over the bear, walking in circles before he gets her to the back woods towards his favorite trail. It's almost dark the sun is so low. Perfect riding weather. And he's wearing that navy fleece with our old stable's name across the front breast. They are one—like people say about men and horses. The bear's face has changed; she is no longer the long-faced eater I see her as in the back pasture. He reaches down to stroke her back, and she rocks her head slightly.

"It's beautiful, Dad, really," I say to him. He turns from looking at the pasture.

"What is?"

He's not seeing it like I am. What can he see?

"The bear," I say. "You and her. It's beautiful."

I've Decided

I am scared of tomorrow morning's MRI
although I said I wasn't.

They will scan
my brain, spine
seeking tumors growing or
bone-secrets asleep in
crevices.

I've decided being so still
will be macabre
but I won't fold my hands
as the metal sings around my
head, my body.

I've decided I want
a biodegradable urn
to hold my ashes deep
in the soil   back home
quiet, wet, and dark
where I will   grow
into a cherry tree
shedding pink petals
in the air
come windy spring.

JENNY FERGUSON

Yes, I Gave Him Mono. Once: A Monologue with Shared Saliva

He tells me I am the kind of person who kills other people so I cry.
The fresh pine car smell dangles from his mirror, stings my throat—still the
    smell is real and familiar even in his car where there are no trees.
I come from a strictly plastic Christmas tree kind of family.
And I haven't climbed branches in years, not since I got boobs.

I'm trying to hold a straight face when he tells me he dates thirteen-year-old
    girls instead of girls like me because they are just like mosquitos at a
    summer fireworks show.
It's my birthday and I'll cry if someone calls me a killer.

He tells me I am the kind of person who kills other people so I cry under my
    pillow because I remember a grade school teacher I liked with
    particular abandon suggested learning through osmosis at night.
I admit I'm not a very good driver, but that's not what he's talking about.
He's not a very good driver either, one hand out the window, tapping a beat
    on the window frame, one hand resting on my thigh, steering with his
    knees.
He's like spit on a birthday cake.
He can't help what he leaves behind when he exhales.
Because that's what happens when he's too cheap to buy his own pop at the
    mall, when he sits too close to me in those plastic booths every lunch
    hour and knocks his knee against mine, how can I say no?

Because Magnolias Predate Bees

They relied on beetles to crawl through
their creamy blooms then track the goo
deep into that cute tree down the hill.
And pay no mind to botanists who
classify that dance as *dumb pollination*
just because beetles lack workers, queen bees.
They don't need any stinking hierarchy.
They serviced magnolias through ice ages,
droughts, the great post-meteor die-off,
good soldiers mucking hip-deep through sex juice,
its sucking sweetness perhaps odd at first,
like a boy's first touch of his own semen
while breathless, his heart still in gear.

What is this? The boy asks, pumped from so deep,
now webbed across his fingers
like nothing he has ever felt before,
wet yet silken. Not that the boy is dumb,
although he will be a pollinator.
But for now there's another new thing—guilt.
Should he refrain? Perhaps impose limits?
Twice a week? Once? No, that's far too harsh.
Here is a transportation. There can be no retreat.
His role in the grand promenade's revealed—
to propel this stuff with all tails swishing,
the sight that stressed poor van Leeuwenhoek
in 1680s Delft because, before
he could announce his great find, he had to
swear his specimen came from coitus.
He had to swear he had not been doing
the thing which could not even be spoken.
In the name of science he had pulled out.

Before I Was Fully Awake

"Sleep, those little slices of death"
—Poe

Kathy had already told me her dream:
   a baby had crawled up in our yard,
and she had changed its diaper
   before asking me what we should do.
I said, "We have to take it to the pound."
   Or at least that's what she said I said.
I knew she wanted to be the star
   of her own dream so I let it go,
how she'd referred to the baby as *it,*
   something I could have nailed her on
were this one of our playful quarrels.
   But it was early, and I was foggy,
still slow from last night's wine and Benadryl,
   my most productive hours (they all say)
given again to a glacial recovery,
   that series of recalibrations
humans undertake after those hours
   spent in whatever sleep is, don't ask me.

It's like they drift into little trances,
   say the alien anthropologists
as they observe our nightly lie-downs.
   Their life-force has no notion of sleep
so it intrigues them how we go willingly,
   even looking forward to the state.
This is a brainy science-fiction film,
   not the usual us-versus-them business
where robots, death-rays, even
   babies crawling up out of nowhere
unite our kind against a common threat,
   the brave standing tall, changing a nappy,
the craven often fleeing to their doom.

In this film though, field notes are taken,
theories advanced on us, the subjects
    who ever so slowly shake off our trance
and perhaps share a dream before
    going straight back to discussing the cat.

When I Hear Buck Owens Sing "Hello, Trouble"

I know it's been decades since the last time
this song came through a radio speaker,
thrilled me with Buck's best line ever—
how right after his welcoming, "Come on in,"
Buck says, "We'll make a pot of coffee,"
(what's known in fiction as the *telling detail*)
because a mere cup just won't suffice
when *Trouble* itself shows up, sits down,
when it's circa 1960 Bakersfield
and hospitality means Maxwell House
percolated till bitter, slurp-sipped
over ashtrays stubbed with Camel butts,
the red and white checked oilcloth
corner-torn near indelible jam stains,
all in the leaden air of eternal bacon,
what one breathes in this linoleum kitchen
where the descent from ruddy childhood
to lower working-class has played out.
Here a stack of past due bills. There a summons.
Plus someone's been cheating, of this we're sure.
And the Chevy's rear main seal, thought to be fixed,
has gone back to dripping, the whole tableau
predicting Ray Carver's morose couples,
beat-down and hung over yet still gabby,
a generation with no war to go fight
given to drink, rock bottom as normal.
And look who just showed up,
settling in with, *Thanks, I take mine black.*

COLON FOXWORTH

Civic Duty

ARNOLD ADAM LAY STRAPPED on the gurney, an IV tube in his arm. They had come for him earlier, taking him from his pod to the Science Center. His electronic handcuffs and leg irons had been removed quickly. The attendants were efficiently preparing for the procedure.

Adam looked up at one of the attendants, a young woman with a chestnut brown eyes peering sharply over her surgical mask. He decided to tell her what was on his mind and in his heart.

"I don't want to do this! I know I agreed..."

"Inmate, you've got no choice. It's your sentence," replied the attendant in a terse voice.

"I've changed my mind! How can you do this? You have medical ethics!"

"Inmate, your sentence has been approved by the Council. Our oath is to the nation-state. "

"But, what about my *life!* It won't be improved, it'll be over! That's assuming it even works!"

"The procedure works, inmate. It's been tested numerous times. Our technology to preserve the life functions when facilitating the transplant is exceptional."

"It won't be me!"

"It will be your body. That's you. Your brain and its functions, desires, and memories are being disposed of here today. You will receive an acceptable brain which serves a vital purpose for our glorious nation-state."

"That's only because I agreed! I've changed my...I want to speak to my attorney!"

Another attendant, a short man, spoke rapidly. "The recent amendment to the Constitutional Charter abrogates the right of counsel for people convicted of crimes such as yours." He paused. "Plus, the Council forbids you to have any contact with your previous attorney, friends, or family. It's not productive."

"I didn't think this through! I don't want the transplant! I didn't do anything wrong!"

"You were a Negative Producing Citizen without exemption. The nation-state made that status a crime decades ago."

"I can change! I'll make more money, just give me another chance!"

The man said, "You had the five year redemption period after your initial warning. It's too late. It's time for you to produce a positive return for our nation-state."

"The Council graciously allowed you to contribute your production by this program. In barbaric times, you might have been imprisoned," added the female.

Adam was suddenly resigned to his future. It had sounded better than being stripped of his citizenship and banished from the nation-state forever. He had assumed that having a new brain would make him smarter, not eradicate all his memories and replace his thoughts. He should have asked more questions, but he had faith that the Council knew best. It was in the Charter. No matter what Adam's faults were, he had always followed the law to the best of his knowledge.

"I guess you're right." he said. "Will this hurt? Is there any chance I will remember anything?"

The man answered. "Your cognitive functions will cease immediately upon injection of the preserving sleep agent. We will simultaneously prep the replacement organ so the implantation will take place quickly, reducing the odds of rejection."

"So, my body and soul wake up if everything goes well, but my mind will be asleep?"

The woman spurted, "Science has officially rejected the existence of a soul! There is no quantifiable evidence. As such, the Council has banned discussion of it. You should know that."

"Sorry." Adam paused as they worked. "You said my cognitive functions stop. Can I dream?"

"The research on that is inconclusive."

"Is it possible, at least?"

"Theoretically. We make no promises. The Council forbids guarantees not firmly rooted in accepted scientific research. The most likely scenario, given what we know, is that you'll have the same awareness as prior to your birth."

"Meaning nothing?"

"You could put it that way." The female attendant answered with no emotion.

"My brain will be kept, right? There's a chance it could be used in the future, right?"

The man spoke to the woman. "We're almost ready to proceed with extraction and implantation." To Adam he said, "It's unlikely. The Council hasn't yet approved implantation of an NPC brain into a Volunteer Undesirable Citizen. However, the preservation module will keep your brain for two centuries, by Council rule. Things could change, but don't count on it."

Adam's thoughts flickered as the attendants finished preparation. The drug that flowed through his veins made him sleepy. He knew it wouldn't be long now. Maybe they were wrong. Maybe he would retain his memories with a new brain in his body. Maybe one day his brain would be used in another body. It was possible. He just hoped he would dream while he slept. Of course, he wished for happy dreams.

The Director came in and stood over Adam. He had a piece of paper in his hand and wore the regal brown uniform of his advanced level within the nation-state. Adam's gaze was losing focus but he heard the initial words clearly.

The Director said, "Inmate Arnold Adam, having been charged with the crime of being a Negative Producing Citizen as the value of your production being less than the value of what the nation-state provided for you; and having confessed your guilt thereto; and having agreed to the implantation of a suitable brain in your body for a purpose that will benefit the productivity of the nation-state; the procedure ordered by the honorable Council To Improve The Nation-State will commence at the conclusion of this statement.

The brain to be implanted in your body is that of a multilingual criminal proficient in arson and explosives. The purpose of combining this mind with your body is counter-espionage in a country hostile to our nation-state. The Council recognizes your dedicated citizenship in this regard. You are officially pardoned for your productive deficiency. Your family members, both living and your descendants, will have the demerits in their files expunged. Our nation-state is grateful. You've done your civic duty."

Arnold Adam smiled with pride as the last sentence was spoken.

KATHERINE FRAIN

Harriman State Park, Virginia

Once I saw a tree feathered by green
leaves and the black hands of lightning.
This was not the miracle, the way ash
can run thick with sunlight and spring.

This was only the way that grief freezes
the body. A neck wet with salt, a girl
written in dust. The miracle is the boy

we nearly called Moses, but named
Sugar instead. For his mistakes
and the answering confusion of sweetness.
This isn't God. This is him at the honey-

locust, waiting for wind and the splintering
bones in my shoes. Because the trail
is a reliquary. Because the world persists

in the determination of moths
trying to lift a flashlight's fallen star, in how
we orient ourselves by what burns. Blackened
legs. Because I never told the miracle about the dead

girl I carried on my back for forty miles, her bad
heart his answer. Because his smile was a coin
buried in the roots of a sky-struck ash,
undervalued and lost and shining with rain.

Appositives

A martyr in ecstatic bloom—air white waves
of ephemera—stranded on the island
of God, transient, heart immaculate,
complete.

Phlox laden with heavy scent,
nameless fields under moonlight,
stars, dawn over the pinewoods,
light from the yellow
iris, brush dry as old
bones, the plundered
flesh.

A gull's refrain echoes in my sleep,
lit windows beckon the children of fable,
red fox lurking, memories—
salt in a wound, silver
fish that slip away.

A willow's erotic sway ripples
the air, always the shore
beckons in my dreams,
a shallow breath is borne
to the singing
wind—the captive
secret—artifact of the past,
light on water, birdcall.

Can I abandon self for once?
Who will remember me?
Watchful mountains in the distance,
I utter my name to the darkening clouds.

D. DINA FRIEDMAN

What My Mother Never Said

Draw more sailboats, another yellow sun.
That smiling orange girl with the flipped up do,
she looks just like you. Don't ever cut your hair.
Draw the blue waves. Find the inky spot
hiding in the squid. Dip your finger in, blot
the white walls. Don't worry
about the radio, its drone of crime, disaster.
Superstition matters. Step over all the cracks.
You look beautiful—that crooked hair. Sit
on my lap. Get a blue tattoo. Believe
in Rorschach, all those inky lies.
Don't give us any news. Tell me
about the scrapes of your day,
so I can stroke your hair.
You will have a happy life.

Views on the Interpersonal Significance
of Nerve Growth Factor

SHE HAD RECENTLY upgraded her breasts for her husband. She had gone from her natural white Caucasian C-cups to a slightly darker pair of D-cups. This included a change from her original pink nipples and areolas to dark brown nipples and areolas. So it had been an upgrade in both size and type.

Her husband had been growing remote, foreign. A kind of tight-lipped hardness attended him wherever he drifted through the house, sometimes encountering her on the stairs or in the bathroom. In addition to her husband's distance, her discovery of his esoterically named folder of downloaded porn on the computer they shared had prompted her decision to go through with the breast augmentation.

When her husband saw her new larger, darker breasts he expressed his approval by gripping them in his hands and shifting them around on her chest like gaming joysticks. He took them in his mouth and made wetly affectionate sucking and popping noises. He was very pleased. He kissed her on the lips and said, "I love you."

And she was relieved, for a time. But her husband eventually became as disinterested with her new breasts as he had with her old ones, and his remoteness returned. So she had another procedure done, this time replacing her pink lips with slightly darker lips, to match her breasts. However, her husband found this augmentation only mildly compelling. She then replaced her long nose with a wide, bridgeless nose. This proved much more captivating to her husband. He touched her new nose in bed and said, "You're finally starting to become the woman I always knew you could be."

It came to fruition that she replaced not only her entire natural body with manufactured body parts, but her personality as well. She had her sense of humor augmented to a more generous sense of humor; her code of discipline to a more strict code of discipline; her intelligence to a keener, more penetrative intelligence. Her husband had always accused her of being deficient in these areas, so she paid to have them improved. Her husband, however, found these new improvements distressing, because she was now no longer the person he had fallen in love with. He told her in their bedroom, "You're improved but no longer you," and began packing his belongings. While he packed, she pleaded with him not to leave; she trailed him through the house and told him she could change back if that's what he wanted. But he said it didn't matter anymore what she did, because he had fallen out of love with her and could never fall back.

So he left. And it wasn't long before she had a final procedure performed: she replaced her head and face with her husband's. The reasons for her going through with this procedure were complex and obscure even to herself, but at least in this way whenever she saw her reflection, she knew she would always have someone she loved staring back.

Cassandra, Late to the Party

doesn't want to be here. She shifts uncomfortable
from left toe to right heel in dainty ill-fitting shoes,
adjusts the straps of her silk shift.

Because, who wants to be that girl,
bringing bad news after the claxons have already
gone off, everyone evacuated, safe and relieved

once the emergency's over? She may know too much
about each party guest to make small talk;
this one, plagued with a fatal tumor she doesn't even see yet,

that one, unaware of his increasingly weak heart
straining to laugh at someone's joke.
It's tough to smile and be silent, when no one

invites her to sing at karaoke, no one asks to buy her a drink.
She's known to be chilly, a downer, clumsy with words
with no wild side. Her wild side tamped down

long ago under circumstances no one here could imagine.
And she knows her own end, too, what it's like to lose
a bet with a God who said he loved her.

Mumblings

Again he had put his hand in the bear's mouth
But the bear was bored having just eaten a whole town
So he took to lugging sacks of potatoes to his still
More than he could use and they became wormy
The mist of allegory would come that night
To suffocate those susceptible to inspire those
Already inspired to further condolences of the past
It was more than he could take so he went for a swim
Cut a hole in a frozen lake and immersed himself
Until he was barely alive got out and ran naked
To the house of a friend who always had a fire
And animal skins thrown about and ready for use
He was a hunter of few words that liked to sing dirty songs
And so it went through the night until the vodka would no longer go down
And they slept where they sat and dreamed their separate dreams
And the embers mumbled their red mumbling about something
That was really a thing about something else
And the bear having grown hungry again
Came nosing about

MICHAEL GASPENY

Hadassah's Property

1. A Little Detergent

Before you went to the Hebrew home,
husband in the ground, losing your mind,
you begged me for help in mailing
a mini-box of Tide containing two pebbles
of soap to Merlina, a teenaged friend in Athens
who'd gone up the chimney at Auschwitz
along with all your family
after Hitler strangled Greece.
Had you forgotten she was ash
or did you hope detergent could bring her back?
The ads did promise miracles.

We couldn't mail the soap,
not even to the North Pole.
The cellophane tape you applied thirty years ago
was peeling and car wash coupons
made insufficient postage. You were shrieking
in Greek. I took the Tide, held you, and promised to handle
the details. This facsimile is the best I can do, air-mail,
requesting confirmation of delivery.

2. A Pool of Shadows

Once, a photo of your family picnicking
appeared in the *Morning Star*—
forty or so souls and you
with a circle around your head
identifying the only survivor.
What it must have cost to wear.

You told me you lurched awake each night,
sure your mother lay downstairs
on the carpet below the menorah.
You always tried to hug the shadows
whose emptiness made you gasp.
In August, the carpet throbbed like a fever.

What if your yearning came true
and she'd been there breathing—
twenty-five years younger than her daughter?
How could you explain?

3. A Ruined Arbor

In sunny weather, you and beloved Nikos lounged
under backyard maples at a wrought-iron table
shaded by an umbrella and surrounded by day lilies.
But fierce Nikos never relaxed for long.
With your matching blue numbers in the buttery light,
he told the same death-camp stories
as if you'd never heard them and hadn't been there,
as if, told often enough, they might shatter.
"Nikos, please stop," you begged,
half from love, half from caution.
You felt the other neighbors edging farther away.
Even so, for you both, joy was this arbor.

Now the table rusts; the umbrella has burst;
the undergrowth has eaten your flowers.
Wisteria wreathes Nikos' bower.
In April, the lavender blossoms around the table
nodded in the breeze like witnesses honoring
Nikos' wrath till they couldn't hold on any longer.
Those fluttering petals seemed superior to human beings.

A few years before you left,
the jungle took the yard.
You refused my help.

4. A Throne

One April morning, you and Nikos strolled
down the street, giddy in the breeze,
each holding the arm of a lawn chair
plucked from a neighbor's refuse.
It didn't matter the backrest was shredded,
exposing aluminum ribs. The find disappeared
inside the garage till Nikos died. Then you placed
the chair among gray leaves at the back fence
facing your kitchen window. Its hungry look

chilled me till the metal blazed in dusk's glare.
You had chosen the spot with care.
I saw Nikos ruling there.

A few years later, kudzu choked the chair
and sealed your back door.
You didn't speak of Nikos anymore.

5. An Accusation

So many autumns after Nikos died,
we raked leaves in our front yards,
teasing back and forth to make time fly:
"You're invited to the Leaf-Rakers' Ball," I called.
"No, my friend, the band plays here. Come dance."
"Dassah, how can you go inside without helping me?"
"Tomorrow, bright and early, I'll ring your bell, Sleepy Head!"

This morning, as I raked, your echo drove me
to an accusation you had too much faith to make—
If God cannot deliver the soap,
spin shadows into your mother,
place you and Nikos on a throne
above an arbor of stars,
then what was any breathing for,
most of all, first breath, first tide?

I Have a History of Falling

for beauty. Once, climbing stone steps out
of a cavern, I couldn't help but gaze
at sun reflected off river, and down I went.

When cathedral bells lured me to count
spires, and I fell face forward in gravel,
my nose unspooled blood onto my coat.

Carrying one last river rock to complete my garden,
I glanced at purple sage lush with bees, and slid
on the wet slope—ankle, fibula and tibia broke.

But today, only stunned knees beneath snow-melt
on a bare branch. And who witnessed my blunder
on black ice? Only the naked elm.

Museum Piece—Naples 1906

HER FATHER'S bloody body was dumped into the Fontana del Gigante by Russomanno clan henchmen. They'd murdered her older brother the month before. The Zangaras of the Torre Annunziata district of Naples were decapitated. After the funeral, Giulietta Zangara sat, pale, her black hair clutched in her fists.

Her young nephew, Ignazio, brought her a blood orange juice. "What will you do?"

Giulietta raised her head. She sighed. "I'm taking over as *guappo*."

Ignazio stiffened. "No woman has ever led a Camorra family. You'll be challenged."

Giulietta straightened, and her eyes hardened. "Dispatch the *soldati*. My father will be avenged."

In the baroque church, gold ampoules of San Gennaro's dried blood miraculously liquefied on his feast day confirming the Saint's protection of Naples, but this year the blood remained coagulated. Vesuvius began to smoke, and confessionals were better attended than bars. Giulietta insisted that her niece say bedtime prayers.

The eruption started as a cloud of ash that spread across the sky like a giant cedar shot through with brilliant lightning flashes. The first lava was a red slash across the throat of the mountain. The earthquake that followed threw Giulietta's Murano vases to the travertine floor. Boulders and pumice spewed from the crater and thudded atop Torre Annunziata homes. Priests locked churches for fear of a cave-in. A *boca* gaped open on the shoulder of the mountain and out shot a geyser of lava. A ropy-surfaced river of orange crushed houses in its path and threatened Torre Annunziata.

Ignazio, burst into the living room. Giulietta sat in an armchair, knitting. "*Zia,* it's time to go."

Giulietta's eyes rose. The knitting needles clicked.

Ignazio's voice was loud. "The sky is electric. The sea is boiling. People have ripped open the doors of churches and carried away saint statues for protection. Cries to God echo everywhere."

A boulder hit the wall of the building with a crack. Ignazio jumped. Outside Giulietta's window, the billowing gray sheet of ash eclipsed sunlight, and the afternoon darkened like midnight.

Ignazio said, "There's a foot of ash on the street muddied by the rain. It's as sticky as chocolate. We need to go before it's impossible to get away."

"No."

"Why are you waiting?"

An explosion from the mountain boomed like a hellish clap of thunder.

Giulietta smiled. "If the lava buries me, two thousand years from now I'll be a plaster cast inside a glass display." She pointed at the floor. "My broken vases will become priceless artifacts in a museum."

Ignazio raised his hands. "What are you talking about?"

Zangara put down her knitting. "Ignazio, if I show fear, the Russomannos will be emboldened. After I stand against Vesuvius, no man will think to intimidate me. *Capisce?*"

Ignazio blinked. He nodded.

"You can go."

Ignazio swallowed. He sat on the chair beside Giulietta. "I'll stay."

She patted his hand. "You'll be a great *guappo*." She returned to her knitting and smiled. "Unless you become a museum piece."

ADAM GIANFORCARO

Crying Glass

THE DRUGS KICK IN earlier than I want them to, so I pull over and sit in the shoulder for a couple hours. The sky is soft and tastes of sweat. I twirl it around my fingers, curl clouds behind the windshield. My hands dance like they mean it. The sun, low and falling.

A semi flashes by, shimmies the car. I zone back in. I shake my head a little, look at my hands. I figured they'd have some dye on them, some cotton-candy, sunburst ooze. But they don't. Just my old hands and hairy knuckles. I want to save this moment—must!—so I struggle to get the phone from my pocket, slide to unlock, find the camera icon. I watch the colors blur on the screen. They move like *Starry Night*. I snap the picture with unsteady hands. Muted hues. Grainy and pale. I put the phone back in my pocket.

I sit there a bit longer, just squinting into the sky. I have this strange moment where I pray a little. I feel myself mumbling, the air coiling around my lower lip and tickling the ends of my mustache.

"God," I say. "A sunset. A child." I don't say anymore. He knows what I mean. He being Him and all.

And I feel it. See it even. My prayers answered. The warmth of a figure between my legs, naked and moist, mutely present with eyes wide and dark. I know, I know. It takes several months for sight to develop in a newborn. And a man can't technically give birth. I get it. But this sky is magical. The colors allow for the impossible—touching the child's eyes as Jesus had done to beggars. It's that kind of sky.

And just when I feel the joy in my chest, in my throat, just when I think the moment is perfect, the crying starts. The infant's eyes spit streams of glass all over my lap—colors, prisms—a small world in those tears. Remnant reflectors. Brimming domes of royals and rose. The sky pinkens outside my windshield, and more and more the sky pinkens in those mirrored tears. Domes inside domes. Matryoshka dolls crying salt, crying sand, crying glass.

It's all too much to handle. I really shouldn't've taken that third hit.

A pick-up pulls over several yards in front of me. I force myself to zone back in, if only for a second. I brush glass from my lap.

Jesus Christ, I think.

I look to a man rushing towards me. He is a young man, blonde and wearing over-alls. He pulls a phone from his breast pocket. I think he's going to put it to his ear, call an ambulance, but he doesn't. He just extends his arms with phone in hand.

"That sky," he says. "It's magnificent."

I wipe my brow. I can't tell if the colors on the back of my hand are bits of sky or blood. I think I hear sirens, but it could be man's radio blasting through the open door.

"Pure beauty," the man says. "God is great."

D. A. GRAY

Aubade: Monk's Pond

Before the cidered glow creates
the world again, two stumble.

Measured steps of blind petitioners
demand proof and night's fingers
discover, in turns, the velvet of loam,
cuts from sycamore root and briar,

or waking,
                marvel how a warm sachet
of flesh covers a valley of bone.

The world ends on a cold, glass pane.

Stop, she says, I haven't been born.

Murmurings of wild voices echo
and unseen feet create ripples,
drumming slowly beneath the surface.
Light cuts its hue on the whetstone of clouds,
setting water ablaze,
                        severs
the tops of trees from the sky
who weeps at his loss.

In the tears, twin branches plumb downward
and winged arbiters glide on the surface between.

The Gap

an angel told me
my brain has compensated
for the small but growing gap
in my vision
replaced its garish city lights
with new synapses
bypassing the harmful deposits
left behind by the peepshow collective

the spectral face whispered
a path of light
extending from a body of secrets
perhaps chants from a lost canaanite tribe
or Toltec teachings from a timeless elder
waking the dead vision centers of my brain

people are starting to disappear

unearthly lights appear
in unexpected places

war drums fall silent
and call the tribes together

When the Water Goes Bad

His mother's words had haunted him
since he was four years old.
    you must tell the people
    where to find
    water
    when the water goes bad.

In dreams he would stand beside her
outside a white clapboard house
on a hillside
while people in a long line climbed uphill.

She would say to him
    you must tell the people
    where to find
    water
    when the water goes bad.

Then she vanished from sight
as the first clump of climbers approached
right before he awoke.

The steady drumbeat of advancing thunder
becomes louder
something no longer beyond hearing
here before he knew it.
Poison fills the air.
Brittle battle lines draw themselves.
One doomsday dream conjures the next;
a scared people stare skyward for signs.

The rain begins to fall to earth.
    tell the people
    where to find
    water
    when the water goes bad.

The stain seeps into the groundwater.
tell the people
where to find
water
when the water goes bad.

In lucid dreams
he pleads with his mother
to explain,
to show him what he needs,
but she assures him
that he has always known.

MATTHEW HAUGHTON

For a Copper Thief

as told by T. Boggs

Buddy, I'll have you know
I'm part
of these hurting times.
Understand I kept
that old
air-conditioning unit
behind
my shed
to use for spare parts.
It sat there
for close to a year,
until you
appeared
like a scavenger
to pick
its bones clean,
gutting
the thing
for its copper tubing.
You see,
as it happens
I'm not rich.
The wealthy
don't cry over spare parts.

For a Pentecostal Woman, Grocery Shopping

If I can speak beyond
how her hair
is uncut
because of scripture,
there's a balance
to how
she moves
in an ankle-length
denim skirt,
with no give or hem.
I am taken by
the country
of her face,
its quietness
as if stilled
from a childhood
memory—
of pressing
her cheek
to a backseat window,
and watching
coal trucks
tear up
the winding roads
with their
heavy payloads.
She will disappear
behind the produce,
but later
I'll wonder
if she has slid
out from those
bone-white sneakers,
to rest her tired ankles.

MATTHEW HAUGHTON

For the Nudist of Dog Slaughter Creek

It's alright to go naked over there,
for the body
is meant
to be read like a book.
In those shadowed woods,
each limb
seems to snatch
at bare skin,
as if longing
for the smoothness
of flesh
to pass over branch tip.
If you follow that body
deeper in,
best you behave
as it does.
Mimic how it moves,
sly amongst
the nettles.
For the body is knowledgeable,
made aware
of its environment.
It has learned to take
the sun
into its stomach,
to expand
within itself
when resting in the tall grass.
It knows
every nook in the path,
every cranny.
Every briar stand and creek bed.

Dairy Freeze

Eula Mae Jones looks out the sliding
window of the Dairy Freeze at the children

sitting in rows as the school bus
slows to drop them off across the street.

Like every school day, yellow lights flash,
then red ones, then a stop sign on hinges deploys

from the side of the bus like a prohibitive
hand so there is no mistake about it.

And even with all that, a red Jeep Cherokee flashes
by in the passing lane forcing three girls crossing

the street to freeze in front of the bus as if on the edge
of a cliff, the wake of the Jeep ruffling their dresses.

Eula Mae lowers her hands from her eyes
and hails the girls over to the window

for a free chocolate cone to celebrate the
wonderful day they lived to see tomorrow.

Bouree

"THEY AIN'T goin' let him go. I can feel it in my throat." Miss Kitha shifts restlessly in her rocker. "They ain't never goin' let my baby out that place." She smoothes wisps of coarse black hair from her temples, matting them with her sweaty palms.

"Hold back, Miss Kitha. You don't know what the Good Lord got in store." Jilly presses his big, flat hand on the woman's shoulder then leans down and hugs her close. "Flotreece ain't had no business gettin' you all worked up. They just got to look at the facts some more is all."

"You know damn good and well my Bouree ain't done what they said he done. He ain't never hurt a soul in his life—and most 'specially no child. He love children. Always did." Another strip of knotted hair needs readjusting.

"Miss Kitha, it ain't no good cryin' and worrin' so 'bout what's already done. You got to have faith in the Lord that He goin' set things right."

The woman's porch rocker stops dead. She rubs her eyes with her dirty apron and stands erect. "They ain't goin' hang my sweet baby for somethin' he ain't done!" A look of cold determination swells her face as her mind slips into some dark recess.

The sun squeezes jagged shafts of fresh light through the troubled sky, suddenly capturing Kitha's attention again. "You see that tree yonder, Jilly? That sycamore tree next to the shed? My Bouree tied that old tire to the limb so the children could swing on it all day."

Jilly remembers the day Bouree climbed the stout trunk and strung up the tire. He stares intently at the swing, his mind now crowded with images of his friend pushing all the little children—especially Callie—and giggling like a child himself. He would push little Callie tirelessly, regaling her with tales of imaginary animals and pretty angels. It was the children that gave him life. Jilly recalls too that it was he that came along behind Bouree cleaning up the messes when a whim struck him in the head.

"You go down to that jailhouse, Jilly, and you tell them my Bouree don't know where that poor child gone." Fresh tears puddle and burst into streaks across the woman's worn face. "I can't let them take my Bouree from me. He ain't right—but he ain't evil neither."

Jilly flinches. "I'm goin', Miss Kitha," he calls back repeatedly, shaking mud from his brogans with every step. "I'm goin' on down there and see what they doin' with him."

It is a long trudge to town, marked by slosh and splatters from passing wagons and mud-painted cars. Rains had saturated the flat landscape with a watery veneer left glistening in iridescent splotches of sunlight. Jilly is met curtly at the courthouse steps by a deputy.

"You ain't welcome here, Jilly," the deputy calls out. "Bouree can't have no visitors until the judge says so."

"He ain't got no lawyer I can talk to?" Jilly yells back.

"Lawyer's done talked to Bouree, Jilly!" the deputy replies. "You done been told you ain't welcome, so turn it around."

Jilly stands dead still for a spell, staring up at the deputy and the hall of justice, pondering what might be brewing within its walls. At length, he turns and begins retracing his arduous trek. Beads of sweat radiate from his face and forearms, his overalls and shirt in need of wringing from the heavy steam of late August.

The shortcut across the barren fields can do no harm now, he presently decides. Early cotton has all been picked and hauled to Baton Rouge, leaving the humped rows ready for spring tilling. But it will be a sad and lonesome walk home, what with rejection behind him and the burden of sorrow for Miss Kitha ahead—he brings no new information for all his trouble.

A sudden gust of warm air, accompanied by heavy rain, sweeps unimpeded across the open field now, dissolving the barren rows of earth like mounds of sugar. It is the first heavy rains and battle of the elements since picking time. The dark skies streak, and rolls of thunder send field mice and a pair of menacing coons skittering toward the woods. At field's end, the live oaks and chinquapins interlace and shelter creatures from the threatening storm. Jilly, too, huddles and huffs under the welcoming canopy.

It is here, this very spot, where Jilly and Bouree played as children, hid up trees from angry pursuers. Bouree loved to watch Jilly shoot his .22 rifle at cans and bottles and field rats in this spot. Jilly recalls Bouree's fascination with his gun and the thrill of bullets finding their mark. "Shoot another one, Jilly!" he'd plead. "Shoot that rat over there. Mama says they eat our food. Shoot it, Jilly!" Bouree would yell repeatedly. His voice still echoes in Jilly's mind. Bouree was always amused by the simplest of things.

On the opposite side of a small clearing stands the giant oak tree they would climb, the muscular arms they'd swing from. It was here they made their plans and pacts, shared their secrets—secrets that dissolved from Bouree's memory by day's end.

But there is a new feature in the landscape as well, something Jilly had not seen before. Beyond the bushes lays a patch of disturbed earth, not unlike that of a burrow thrust upward by local groundhogs. A dark hump of gumbo soil stands swollen and pitted and swirled, as if recently stirred by some unnatural force. The rains have erased any evidence to the contrary. Jilly stares at the anomaly, pondering, first the notion of a tornado touching the earth, then the possibility of children at play. He punctures the muddy mound with a heavy stick as if testing its depth. The plunge stops shallow. "It must be the work of children that discovered our hiding place," Jilly ponders. "They done found it and fouled it—our secret spot. Yeah, that's it, Bouree. They done dug this big hole and filled it up just to mess up our special place."

Jilly quickly sets about patching the troubled earth with a cover of leaves and sticks and windfall acorns, blended it all to match the surroundings. "It's all fixed now, Bouree," he whispers, staring into nothingness. "I'll keep a good eye out from now on. Won't let nobody come near our hiding place."

He sits down under the oak tree, tired from work and concern. At length, the rains abate and Jilly pulls himself up to make the second part of his slow walk home. Clouds have begun to fill the late afternoon sky again, reminding him that nothing bright can last. He turns and stares at the giant oak, envisioning Bouree hanging from a massive bottom limb, yelling at him: "Shoot it again, Jilly! Shoot the bad rat! Kill it, Jilly!"

And it is here it will remain, beneath the dark earth where children no longer play. He can count on Bouree to not recall a thing.

Flying at Night

I love flying at night
when the cabin goes dark
and passengers settle in
for the long flight, hunched

with books under their solitary
lamps, or huddled under overcoats,
sleeping in the engine's deep hum.
Then you can look out the window

at the new moon slung like a deer
rib in the black sky and down
at the lights of tiny towns blowing
like sparks across the darkened plains.

RICHARD HEDDERMAN

Midwinter Vigil

The wind smells like nails.
In the North, clouds

lower their heavy kettles.
The sky is chalk, the roads

carbon; their salts abrade.
Light glances off snow. Sound

travels farther over ice. Numb
to the wrists the copper beeches

retreat into their cells. Sparrows
squall and scatter across the snow

where the wind scrawls its wild name.
The jawbone of the moon drops

as the hourglass scuttles its grains.

RICHARD HEDDERMAN

Winter Mailboxes

They lean into the wind
these Quonset huts of silence,
satellites of winter's news

tilting on their bare axes
and shuddering on a decaying orbit
of light. Countless snows

have blasted them, winter rains
pound their rattling armatures.
The battered doors creak on rusted

latches, and the new moon
is a chalk mark in the black
sky as you reach into that vast,

echoing cavern for the circulars,
the dead letters, for the late
evening news and mail.

Balancing the Books

Sound is a star I hang onto when night balances its books.
In dreams, I polish the stone of myself in the clear water of memory.

You once spoke of loss, how it subtracts.

Didn't we believe our marriage was more than a tithe,
that we would always be together?

The salve of my heart is bone-meal,
and the tightrope I walk keeps me steady.

We paid for what we got.
Too bad it was so little.

To Nuance or Not to Nuance

I

The men I worked with at Folsom Prison,
walk single line
down the knife of night,
their eyes averted,
their blue jeans and shirts
baggy as pajamas

They could be on their way
to chapel,
Bibles in their hands,
and who knows what
in their back pockets

II

My drama instructor knows the poetry
of the body, each nuance a shift of expression;
he lifts the sloping shoulders of a prisoner,
teases the mouth into a frown:

...I could be bounded in a nut-shell and count
myself a king of infinite space, were it not that I
have bad dreams.

III

In my dream, I am a frog leaping into heaven,
a moth perched on my tongue—
cool lake water glistening
off the green which is my frogness
Oh, Holy Father of leaping things
give me dominion over myself,
as well as those that have trouble
finding hope's illusive pond

Please bless these men who remain
chastised by public curse, by accusations,
some of which are legally true

IV

I once thought trouble
a blight on the spirit,
but trouble is a shape-shifter;
it smiles like an angel,
but dresses in shadowy garb

V

"Hamlet is like ballet,"
said the inmate in Arts in Corrections.
"How so?" I ask.
"It's all such delicate stuff."

Ars Poetica

It's Arkansas, not Tennessee.
I dig your accent, too. It's hot.
Hello? I'll try to help you see:
Athletic build, green eyes, big smile,
and, waist-long hair. I'm five foot three,
and only have a necklace on.
So tell me what you'd do to me.
I'll be your personal Grand Prix.

My hand is moving up my thigh.
It's like you're here in bed with me.
What's wrong? You're sounding kinda shy.
It's cool. I'll say the words for you.
Relax. We'll talk till we untie
that tasty candy tongue of yours.
(I'm somethin' new to every guy.
I had this one dude start to cry.)

So whatcha like to do and eat?
It must be me! I'm right? For real,
I've heard you should cut back on meat.
But I don't know. I'm such a blonde,
believing every blog and tweet
like I should be in Spinal Tap.
I love it, too. It's so off-beat.
You know, your laugh sounds really sweet.

To Someone Contemplating Suicide

I can't explain the world or say
a word where physics are concerned.
But I know birds don't lose their way,

that grass grows back when it's been burned,
that caterpillars spring up winged,
and what has died does not return.

Among Gulls

Among gulls
    it is the old who are beautiful,
    rising up from gray-brown,
    inconsequential adolescence
    into the sea air, lords of it,
    cruciform, blazing their white glory.

Mark this
    say I to an old man
    bent like a tree above his own lap
    on the benches along Liffey,
    watching the snow gulls,

writing.

DAVID BRENDAN HOPES

Cocoa with the Gryphons of Nippur

I set down my cocoa. Over the steam
I'm making eyes at the men in the British Museum:
the hurrying fathers, making that sweeping gesture
fathers make to ensure nobody is left behind,
the studious Pakistanis engulfed by raincoats,
the American kids asking after the Rosetta Stone.
If you're here alone, you want something,
and though the fierce stone guardians
of West Asia may be part of it,
they are probably not all. Love
of the terrible stones implies love
of the terrible elsewhere:
the hard assignation, the sharp shadows drawn
by the unembarrassable moon,
a square on the calendar turned suddenly blood red,
the opening overcoat,
the closed hand, which might contain anything.

Wouldn't you kiss him on the hard breast knot
between the opening wings?
Wouldn't you kneel down
under the bending stone eminence, overshadowed,
overcome, with the sound of avalanche,
with the deep animal purr?

Out of Place

When I see my dentist
in his baseball cap and sneakers
walking down the street like a regular guy

without a probe or excavator
or tiny round mirror in his hand;
no rubber gloves, no hygienist

sitting attentively across from him,
anticipating his needs and my needs;
no tasteful prints on the wall,

no Muzak in the ceiling,
no adjustable overhead light—
just the sun shining down on both of us,

and him too far away for me to see
all the little unruly tongues
of his nose hairs sticking out—I don't

recognize him at first,
striding through the world all alone like that,
as if he weren't my dentist, as if

he didn't belong in my dentist's office,
as if he had a life outside
my head. Then he tilts his head and looks

at me askance, as if I were
sitting there in his dentist's chair,
and he gives me a smile that says

he not only recognizes me,
but he recognizes himself
inside my head, where I've been keeping him

prisoner. And he raises a deft hand
and lets himself out
with a wave.

Student Driver

I hate this stalled poem
which has gotten only as far
as the title
written in big letters
on the little billboard
on the roof of the car in front of me,
the two shadowy figures
in the front seat
putting their heads together
over the trundling dumb
progress of this poem. I'm in a hurry,
but the poem is going nowhere and I really
want to help them with it,
because I think I can see
how if they take the next off-ramp
it will be the perfect ending:
happy, easy, clever. But no,
the poem wants to go
somewhere else.
It wants to go where I am going.
And what can I do
but stare straight ahead
at the two heads in the front seat,
while the poem looks back
at the two heads in the front seat
of a different car, an older car,
a rusty green Dodge Dart
on a dusty backstreet
in a time and place
before seat belts were invented—
one head small, curly, mine,
the other larger, heavier, graying,

leaning under the weight
of all that love, all that
history, careful not to condescend
as it leans down, as it leans
lovingly in, beginning to describe, instruct,
praise, delight, and ending
in wisdom.

One Ambition

All I ever really wanted
was to whistle with my fingers.

I knew I would never
be the one up on stage

blowing everybody away
with beauty, brilliance, virtuosity...

But to be the lightning
inside the thunderous applause,

to have the audacity
and the manual dexterity

to make a siren screeching
through a dark auditorium,

to be the killer hawk
in all that parroting, pattering rain,

to be, finally, the very best at praise—
now that was something

I thought that if I gave my life to
I might attain.

True Story

THE TRESTLE MUST have looked huge—wide as a street, its edges concealed in the darkness. I like to think he took the measure of it before shuffling onto the thick wooden beams. And it was built so strong…it could suspend a train eighty feet in the air as it rushed from Göteborg to Malmö, filled with a hundred sleepy faces staring at screens. Surely it could hold a man.

The police asked us what happened and the stories began. He drank, we knew. Snakebites, extra vodka (we assumed, because he often drank those). He met a girl that night, and her name was…Janna? Emma? Well, she had a name, we agreed on that. We also agreed that he came with us to Alek's flat, but then he wasn't there anymore. As to the rest, I let them bicker because everyone was drunk at the time and, besides, no one was with him.

Now I stare up at the lattice of timbers and, above that, the thin line of railroad. He must have seen something more substantial than this thread I see wavering against the afternoon sky. Or maybe it reminded him of a childhood adventure, or he just gave in to an impatient desire to go home, go to sleep? Maybe he walked the rail like a balance beam, trusting in its powerful geometry to ferry him safely to the other side.

Or maybe he knew. Maybe he looked down and saw the mystery and said "fuck it" and stepped into air.

The wind begins to bite, and I pull my jacket closer. Somewhere warmer, his other friends are probably still talking and the police are still taking notes. But facts—real facts—are few.

The cliffs exist; the trestle remains. The rails extend from one side to the other, laser straight, waiting for the grip of wheels. At some moment in the past he fell and at some moment after that he landed, and the dirt, thirsty from drought, slurped at the blood and vodka from the places where he broke. The stain is still here, spread like a shadow. Everything else is a fiction.

JOSEPH HUTCHISON

A Tactical Error

SCOOPING THE FINELY GROUND coffee into the basketed paper filter, Frank understands his tactical error. He chose to put down the dog's food, then go to the bathroom, then make coffee—and now the dog's tail is thumping the floor behind him; the dog has gobbled the food and wants outside: he wants the day to begin, and Frank's coffee-making stands in the way. Clearly Frank should have peed before putting the dog's food down. The shaggy tail thumps like the toes of his wife's shoe when Frank's annoyed her. If she hadn't left the house earlier for her twice-weekly workout at the Y, her toe and the dog's tail would both be punishing the kitchen tile. Now the dog lets go a gruff little moan—his "I have to poop" moan. This error may turn out to be more than tactical, Frank thinks, and in his distraction dumps half a scoop of coffee over the basket edge: the dark brown grains scatter onto the countertop, and some shower down on the floor. "Fuck!" Frank barks and bends down reflexively as if he might intercept the flying coffee grains, which in turn makes him whack his brow on the counter edge. The floor cranks upward behind him like a concrete slab swung by a crane; the back of his head thumps the tile, unleashing a reverberant sloshing sound in his skull. A circle of bruised air shrinks like a sphincter around the kitchen window's brightness, which quickly dwindles and is suddenly swallowed up. For a stunned few moments Frank lies there, listening to the wet licking sound the dog's making. He's licking my face, Frank thinks. He's trying to bring me back.

When his wife returns she finds that Frank has not only stopped thinking, he has apparently stopped breathing. She also finds that Beaucoup, the dog, has managed to consume such a quantity of Frank's blood that he's thrown it all up along with his breakfast; worse, he has planted an imposing pile of red-velvet shit on the carpet, right where the Berber meets the red clay tile. You couldn't have given me a lousy six inches, she thinks and glares at Beaucoup, who cowers now under the dining room table. But all she says out loud is: "Christ, Frank. What a mess."

Poor Bastard

IT HAD BEEN RAINING people for some time, and from the lip of the blown-out window of the ninety-ninth floor, Adolfo was unmoved as the blond-haired man in the apple green chinos and pink polo flashed before him and rotated in slow motion, as if skewered on a rotisserie. Others in his office dashed every which way but up, but for Adolfo, time abandoned its brisk progress and slowed to a dream. Neither was he moved when the falling man's body squared toward him and a shock of envy burned into his face. The face said, "You're safe for the moment, with a solid floor beneath you!"

"Eagle eyes," the doctor had said to the smiling Adolfo in his younger days. "20-8. That's the max for people, by the way. And quite rare."

Adolfo followed the man all the way down till he stopped getting smaller.

Poor bastard. He was dressed well for the occasion.

The instant he'd assessed the situation, Adolfo had formulated a plan. Tether himself to the heavy desk against the outside wall and hang out the window. He'd braided venetian blind and extension cords together, plenty to hold his one hundred and seventy-three pounds. He was in great shape for a man nearing retirement, lifted at the Y, jogged the golf course. Much like his equity portfolio, it had paid dividends. He would not give up his life so quickly. He could bear pain.

He left a brief voicemail with his new wife Leslie, who was a trooper for him, didn't ask too many questions. When his phone stopped working, he gave his reassurances silently to his stepson Chaney, who'd stormed out of the house last night. That would have to stop, but the boy was coming along.

Both were simple messages. He was going to make it home.

It got too hot to bear inside, and he executed his plan, leaned out the window and positioned his body at an angle so the tether supported his weight. In the somewhat cooler outside air, he wedged his foot in the bottom corner of the window frame and gripped the masonry for stability. They'd soon be here with rescue teams.

A woman dropped past his floor, her loose skirt blown over her face, pantyhose sparkling in the sun, high heels secured to her feet. He watched her plunge until she stopped getting smaller and then got a little bigger.

The fallen man in the pink polo lay well flattened on the pavement next to the tall building, which stretched into the heavens. He scanned the building bottom to top with his one open eye, taking measure of the only world left to him. He tried to move a finger. No dice. He observed people far up, leaning out windows, waiting for their moment, as he'd done a minute ago. They ratcheted their heads left and right, as blind people some-times do. Perhaps they looked for a machine to reach out and lay them safely on the ground, or maybe the hand of God if they were inclined that way. The truth of it, that neither of those was forthcoming, was irrelevant. You never jump from lack of imagination. It's only when pain grows more unbearable than the thought of death.

Dust and debris swirled in the air and a light sliver of something rested on his closed eye. His mind turned to his Uncle Christopher's wood shop in Tom's River, an entire weekend at age nine making a spoon for his mother, a pipe for his father. It was their tenth anniversary. He loved standing side by side with his patient uncle, focused only on the two pieces turning on the lathe. Sawdust had coated his jeans and tee, and a small wood shaving stuck to his cheek. His uncle had said, "You look like a tree," and they laughed all afternoon, made the kind of bad jokes he loved. Now he laughed again, silently, as the collar of his polo poked into his face.

He shifted his gaze upward to the thickening smoke and panic-stricken people, observing the scene with clarity. A man moved around outside a window, the man he'd seen as he fell, the one who peered from the hole, holding a rope. A woman came flying by that man, skirt flared upward like flower petals. Then the man hung at an angle next to the window, flapped wildly, and reeled himself in. It must have taken some strength. As the man disappeared back into the opening, he heard a thud on the ground near him. The woman. After a few moments, the man shot out of his window untethered, arms and legs flailing.

Poor bastard. I was pulling for him.

The woman lay close, he was sure. Did her mind still function? Had she seen the man with the rope? Was she also looking up at him? Or did her skirt still cover her face? When he looked skyward again, the hurtling man's blond hair, pink polo, and green chinos registered in his eagle eye and a pulse of comprehension surged in him. The jumper's face beamed and his arms widened as he saw where he was headed. The reclining man silently smiled his welcome, braced himself the best he could.

Just Like That

the man who sold the moon
got a good price

he danced and danced and danced
then danced some more

it was not even mine to sell
he said
i sold it anyway
for a good price
a good price

crowds all around the world gasped and cried
shook their heads and fists and sighed
as they watched the moon hauled away
across the sky

the stars suddenly more numerous
darkness no longer at the edge of what was

Reply to John Dorsey, the Week before Christmas

i won't shave again until this year's passed
grey and grey color my beard

when the holidays are over
i'll be in the same place

squeaky hinges on the doors
clothes patched or well-worn

friends ask about my health
i smile and nod, smile and nod

offer hot coffee or cold water in the morning
cold wine or cold water at night

Yard Sale

Today's roadside tally: one praying possum;
two gray squirrels flattened into stars; a garter
snake looped into infinity's figure eight,
glistening like a pebble of rain. Yesterday
a cottontail vultures were pulling like taffy,
stretching bands of intestines up into trees.

We don't usually leave death around like that.
We don't see it spread like a yard sale across
a lawn. We like to keep it boxed. Father in his
best suit wearing lipstick, for once not able
to laugh it off. They say you get over it but you
never get over it, just a little closer to it every day.

The neighbors named their kid Happy but she is
never happy. Today she's grimacing, the sun
in her eyes. The future's future there on the horizon.
The end of another rope we must knot with
our teeth. Turn a new leaf, we say, but sometimes
we prefer the old leaf, pruning limbs to make room

for more to grow. Watching a cooper's hawk
take a mourning dove mid-air, wing on wing.
How it takes us out of ourselves and closer to
ourselves, dissolving that film. We can't help
but stare as the claws rip through breast bone,
as the bill tears into a still-pulsing heart.

GEORGE KALAMARAS

Hound Dogs They Held

Based on a photograph of William Johnson, Iva Melton, and Laura Bell, African-American Pueblo-area pioneers, Pueblo, Colorado

SIX PUPS. TWELVE floppy ears. Some bloodline from Mississippi or Alabama. On a farm outside Pueblo. How the black man stirred the black given dirt. How the woman and her thigh. Iva—between them—the child at their side. Six beagle pups. Or coon-hounds? It's difficult to tell when they're young. All ear and eye. Twenty-four squirming paws. One pup in each hand of the three, as if their squirming black selves vowed to sniff out raccoon holes of hate, of defeat, only a loving hound could tree. Haystack at William's back, the back he broke breaking earth. Hard. The Pueblo sun was hard. Clods of dirt near a wheelbarrow already cracked to kindling.

Of course the photo's in black and white. Good and evil. This and that. Left hand and right. The two darkest pups in William's arms. His cowboy hat and bandana say he can carry the full weight of black, repeat the way west was wept. Hard but possible. Possible hard. Laura Bell *is* a belle, in stiff white gingham. Down to the ground, her dress says the way was white and dust. Wagon and rut. And now she must biscuit and mutton and hash. She must work the clods white enough to eat and strong her strength to held the man's back. They likely don't agree, like tenses. Present and past collide in the celluloid eye. Though between them, Iva is past, present, *and* perfect, leaning as she does against Laura's give and get-back-to-earth. Against a mama's calm? Iva already knows she'll one day grow. She'll one day tall right out of her skirt and force of it to cover her black twelve-year-old legs in gingham white.

People they held, these hound dog pups, squirming as if they knew. Know. As if more than tenses don't agree. Though how could they sense all the possible blunt of reaching forward to their past? Pain? Scenting their mother's teat, they only know they need the white milk. The sticky of it and sip. Where could she be? What farm? What parts of the arm? What finger might they nip and twitch? What is broken but the wild of a horse in the corral, a tiny burro tired from lugging sand, dozing hunched in sun? And why do William and Iva and Laura not share a name? Like a family already fractured into a land claim. All the possible parts of the farm where a mama dog could hide from the needle-point milk-teeth tooth. Or shade herself, perhaps, beneath cottonwood calm, beating Pueblo back with a late afternoon sway. Of leaves? Of tail? Of wind where the breath won't? It was wind, after all, that brought them west. Wind in the bullets of the blue and the gray. Wind in the sails of the slave ships' salt. In the better world west. Of Kentucky. Of Tennessee. Of the wide-thighed Missouri. Wind in the belly of the crow eating the innards of a coyote dead by sun. By Pueblo hard and ground. *Pueblo,* of course, means village or town. Communal calm. Adobe abode. Is Spanish for *flat-roofed Sundays* or *make the natives pray.*

But William and Iva and Laura are here, there, in every way west. Perfect. Tense. Calm in their now. So far west they're dead. So far dead, they live again in black and white. Hound dogs they held. The dark squirming paw. The white white smudge on a puppy's snout—six, maybe eight weeks out—already sniffing sun for brutal clouds of hard dark rain.

GEORGE KALAMARAS

Wendell Berry Was Always a Grown Man

Based on a photo of Senator Harry B. Hawes of Missouri and his wife,
Eppes Osborne Robinson—with hunting dogs, November 26, 1926

SO I'M LOOKING at the photo and swear it's Wendell Berry holding the shotgun in 1926. I'm confused. Born in 1934, how could he be alive, let alone already married to the woman on his left, also slinging a gun? But I'm sure it's Berry. The way drops of darkness inhabit the field, in hickory-blister and bare branches of sycamore, and plop themselves onto the coats and ears of the dogs. Even the whitest dog has a flash of dark lightning about to enter its left eye, as if—as in all things Berry—seeing is itself a struggle with the dark, especially when one looks with the gaze of what's in the left pockets of the body's intuitive sod. The man's hat, cocked as if to say, *Kén-tuck is not that far from Missourah.* His eyes, spectacled with the struggle of Saturn's dust merging with Mars' mud. His wife's eyes, absent below the rim's hat. Yes, it's the rim of things that shades the way we speak. Some women of that era silent as forks poised in the drawer. Sadly. Even when holding a gun. If you drop a fork, my superstitious Greek grandparents used to say, it means you'll have a visitor. And it will be a woman. What must have been dropped to allow Wendell Berry access to this scene? Was this him in 1926, only to be reincarnated eight years later one state away, through the narrow birth canal, where the lower side-borders of both states meet? Or did the dogs bring over something trembling and thicket-flushed from the other side that our lives can't quite think? Only one of the dogs, it seems, has some hound in it. The ears always betray. Even when folded generations later into the body of a pointer—standing, now, on Berry's immediate right. My own secret hound self also evident in the acute elongation of my own hearing, as if to scent out the death that lies ahead in the animal I seek. But Berry—when his mind is troubled—wants to lie down *among* the animals, not kill, as he says in his poem, "The Peace of Wild Things." I don't believe his wife. I trust her. I already love her. There is something terribly tough in the way she hides a hand in her jacket pocket, as if bullets of possibility lie there, ready to point Berry past the fields of death into farming and the long furrows of verse. The dogs, also looking far ahead, point toward another field where they all must go. It's Daniel Boone all over again, only this time traveling one state east. This time, not hunting bear, nor killing Indians, but dousing with kerosene the bitten parts of the heart to light them, brilliantly, and let them go dark as they turn to ash. Just like Berry. In his poems. In this photo. In the darkness, he says, that is always with us. In Missouri or Kentucky. In husband, in wife. In either of the double barrels of each shotgun they hold. In two or more ways of mouth. Like Wendell Berry being both here in this photo and being another man decades later, farming a field in

Henry County, Kentucky. He kneels, here, in Missouri, in 1926, before he was born, with his wife, among the dogs, not for the camera but for something holier than the photo can allow.

Yard Work

Approaching our wedding anniversary,
we get into a fight. It's always the same argument,
the same wound that, after 30 years, rears up
unexpectedly like a gnarled root hooking our rakes,
stalling our progress. Bent against our work, argument as fresh
and forceful as the wind that whips the garbage bag from its
uncinched grasp, we claw at the ground like two old ghosts
hacking apart the clods. Somewhere far off our love
mourns from a branch, then from a lamp post,
then back to the scrub oak just out of reach. In my wizened
years I unravel an old rope from a chink in the fence,
split its frazzled raffia, then overturn a shovelful of leaves
to find the tender shoots of grass which make me think of buds
in a petri dish, radish seeds perhaps, the fingernails of an infant.
I scrape back the rot, the hateful words, the tears gone down
through the complex ecosystem of soil that receives
and forgets our anger. I believe that something more is living
in the air beyond the clothesline. History, even ours, hangs heavy
in the junipers waiting to be released.

DEBRA KAUFMAN

To the Orange-haired Lady at the Martini Bar

You order another, voice thick with smoke,
boa slipping off your thin shoulders.
Whenever the door opens
you swivel, half-hopeful.
How could I not speak to you,

looking as you do like Aunt Hortense,
who tinted women's hair in our small town?
Her own blazed and curled like fire.
When I asked her once why she laughed so much,
she said, *Hon, it's either that or cry.*

I admire your cocktail ring. *Rubies,* you say,
from an old beau, then add with a wink,
gold tooth shining,
He was a gorgeous scoundrel,
and pop the olive into your wide red mouth.

Shadow Nocturne

You were a skein of nerve, blood from my marrow,
sliver of bone, a silver weave of luminous cloth,

a fire that spread through electric nerves.
Your little core palpated in its fine mesh,

its tremolo of strings could not hold you.
You shrugged off my body and slipped seamlessly,

knife-edge moon in the water, final glide from the womb,
before dissolving into a blossom on the snow.

Against the light I thought I saw your tiny fist,
too quickly pulled back before I could grab you.

Skin-tight storms ripped a trail of fireflies from the sky,
but I remember only the ripe weight of grief, an ocean,

with you curled underwater as if you could breathe
at all from pinched blue nostrils.

Fallen sparrow, tiny creature I could hold in my palm,
I thought I could reach out and kiss your delicate eyelashes

but they were air-brushed with disappearing ink
on a fluttering moth that vanished into the remnants of night.

AMI KAYE

Spanish Moss

Turtles clamber up the roots of a tree hung with Spanish Moss, and the marshes teem with blue herons and egrets. The driftwood floating in the swamp suddenly cuts through the algae, teeth glistening as a giant maw crunches down its prey. On higher ground fiery azaleas festoon the plantation, and crepe myrtles and magnolias delicately scent the summer. Grand oaks usher visitors to a genteel prosperity. On the other side, veiled by Spanish Moss, are those who power the plantations: they arrive on packed ships, corralled like animals, sold as meat. Shackled, starved, weak from beatings and branding irons, working under the eye of the grinding sun, barely living, and dying, in cramped, smoke-filled cabins. How to endure, how to forgive this theft of life? Here they work, behind mosquito-infested swamps, sweat and blood dripping off mahogany skin. Their scars are beyond healing: to feel less than human, to live and die in bondage, to not know choice. From this endless struggle comes the music of ragged grief. All other languages have failed them. Empty the belly of tears, fill the wind with deep-pitched blues, gospel songs in the purest voices, African tales from a Gullah storyteller, hymns of the spiritual Canaan. Their songs vault above the elegant homes, the moss-strung marshes, the hastily dug graves of their dead brethren. They sing with scorched tongues, lungs aflame, throats mellow and pain-sweetened. Their spirits break free; none can shackle their song—it rises so high and wild, it pierces the clouds.

GLORIA KEELEY

Porch Memories

bird songs braid trees
ballerina moths weave
a web of theater scrim
cocktails on the veranda at dusk
hummingbirds—a thousand wings
trees with sails; boats with leaves
good mooring for splinters
ancient punctuation as in crescent moon
sack of grain ripped open
blueberry bushes; baskets of reeds
baby's cradle in the branches
of red sequoia
kisses touch the core of the universe
crows top trees
kiting on their muscular black wings
memories root on our grounds
bonsais grow into horses
crickets wind-chime
deep in the night
fencerow holds ivy
the far off music of Mississippi
planetary, drifting through ears
sudden timpani of thunder
lay low the soil's cold ribs

Knowing the Man by His Grip

Cutting low over the creek grass,
a hawk takes a squirrel by the neck
& carries it into the shadows.
My father once had that grip, his yellow
nails leaving half moons on my skin
for a screwdriver left on the bench,
the garage floor left unswept.

I painted his house in Galesburg
today. A scowl creased his face
as he found trails on baseboards,
brush streaks on doorways,
muttering *goddamns*
as he paused for breaths.

He hooked his right hand to my arm,
forearm muscles taut
under brown spotted skin.
Don't wreck my house, he coughed,
& the shallow pink scallops his fingertips pressed
disappeared as he gave up his grasp.

What Lasts

I remember settling my children on the barrel
of a retired cannon in the city's park,
its hard rubber tires gouged with initials,
for a photograph. What lasts. What doesn't last.

And here on the Potomac, two young girls
pose before a submarine's propeller,
a great steel flower, four slanting petals,
because we need a background for our lives.

Several passersby have said the water's higher
than last time but no one has mentioned
the smooth log drifted in under the rails
that guard the monument, a tree that lived

year by year the way our children do.
It will take a long time for water
to polish it ring by ring into nothing
but I think that's going to happen.

Celebration

A FEW MILES out of town, Julia was finally free of the gnawing discomfort that took up residence in her belly every time she heard David's voice. She stuck her head out of the passenger-side window and shouted I'M FREE headlong into the breeze, a gesture David would despise.

"Stop that," David said from the driver's seat, in his patented irritable tone. It was the first thing he'd said in over an hour, other than all-purpose curses directed at the traffic, so she held onto the pose until his anger started to subside.

This would be the last time she would ever be a passenger in David's car. They were returning from the lawyer's office, where they'd signed the final divorce settlement, ten years wasted. By now she hated every sweet thing about him, every sweet and thoughtful thing.

Her car wouldn't start this morning, and he was the one who kept that old junker running anyway. He insisted on diagnosing the problem over the phone and admonish- ing her for her failure to complete necessary preventative maintenance. She tuned him out halfway through the first sentence. Lectures like this were the cost of his advice.

"Just come get me, OK?"

"It's fifteen miles out of my way, and I'm already running late. Can't you take a cab?"

"I don't have the money for a fifty-dollar cab ride."

She knew an appeal to his cheapness would work even after his kindness had been exhausted.

The lawyers were surprised to see them arrive together, and one of them made a joke about a reconciliation. No one mentioned that they were two hours late. David preemp- tively changed the subject, remarking upon what a festive outfit she was wearing.

"Well, it is a day for celebration," she said.

After the papers were signed, her lawyer offered her a ride, but she decided to go with David because she was sure he knew the way.

She was a little frightened when she realized he was taking the long way home. He had never hit her, but one night he was screaming at her in the sidewalk and their friends said later they were afraid for her.

"You should be afraid for him," she said, but their concern embarrassed her.

She looked over at David, so intently focused on the road and all its insignificant jousting.

"Sorry," he said, as if awakening from a micro-nap. "I guess I wasn't ready to go home yet."

She nodded, and felt terrible for accusing him, if only in her mind. She resisted the urge to rub his shoulder, the only conciliatory gesture she knew.

"Wanna drive around the block a few times?" she said.

"I thought you were in a hurry." He never could resist needling her. "So what are you doing tonight?"

"A lot." She switched the radio over to her station, and leaned against the passenger side window. She couldn't let the day end. Spoiler Alert: From now on, she'd be lonely.

"So how did we do?" she said. This is how it had always been with them; she started conversations, and maintained them until he got bored.

"It was okay, I think. I mean, I did some things I regret. But I think we made the right decision."

"I know. I'm sorry."

And just as soon as that, before she even had time to think, they had arrived at the house he used to live in. They'd be stripping it of furniture soon, showing it to strangers, trying to convince them that they could make a new life here.

"What a day, huh?" he said.

"It feels like we're on some weird kind of date. I won't be inviting you in, though."

"I know. Well, I guess we won't be seeing each other much anymore."

"Can I call you? About the car I mean."

"Yeah sure. You'd probably be better off taking it to a mechanic."

He kissed her on the cheek and didn't invite himself in for dinner. Chinese delivery again, and when she finished eating she called David to thank him for the ride.

J. D. KOTZMAN

Melissa, in a Thousand Words

A PICTURE IS WORTH a thousand words, they say.

This adage, this notion that a single image can tell a story as well as a block of text, never seemed truer to him than when he peeled back the flap of the mysterious manila envelope—sender unknown—slid out the thick sheet of paper tucked inside, and beheld the lurid photograph on its glossy reverse. A digital print of a stark-naked, drugged-out woman, of her, he realized upon closer examination, once his initial shock had subsided.

Brian Jones and Melissa Mansfield first met as bright-eyed undergrads, huddled in the recesses of the student union building, at an open house for the campus newspaper. Back then, other than that they happened to attend the same tiny liberal arts college and share a casual interest in journalism, they had little in common. He'd spent his childhood in small-town suburbia, a cultural wasteland teeming with strip malls, chain restaurants, and dim-witted, overweight inhabitants who had a penchant for bad Hollywood movies and Kentucky Fried Chicken. She, meanwhile, had grown up in the city, raised by an outspoken neo-feminist mother who, from an early age, inculcated her with a deep appreciation of literature and art, with outings to readings, exhibitions, and shows whenever time and budget allowed. Quite simply, she'd seen more, done more, known more than him. You're such a Philistine, she often teased, to his chagrin, whenever he did or said anything she judged as unsophisticated or ignorant. Over time, though, she remolded him, made him more literary, more cultivated, more haut monde. And now, fifteen years later, for all her incessant talk of writing, her much-touted honors degree in English lit, he—not she—boasted the publishing credits and prize nominations. Funny old world, he thought, setting her picture down gently on his antique roll-top desk.

Back then, Melissa did some modeling for photography classes, just to help cover her tuition, she claimed. The concept—her posing nude, on display before what Brian imagined as gawking, hungry eyes—unsettled him. Still, not wanting her to think of him as gauche, as somehow unworthy of her, he didn't object. It was art, after all, he reasoned. But this, he thought now, allowing his gaze to wander back to the disturbing eight-by-ten, this looked cheap, tawdry, nothing like the muted black-and-whites of her lithe, vibrant form he peeked at back then, one morning when she'd rushed off to class and left a set of matte prints behind in his doom room. And she wasn't twenty anymore, wasn't even thirty. She looked like a streetwalking whore, an old, tired, used-up one, he concluded. The harsh simile made him wince. Even now, after all of the fucked-up mind games she'd played over the years, he didn't want to think of her that way.

Instead, Brian conjured up the memory of their second encounter, when he and Melissa happened upon one another by the sangria bowl at a Halloween soirée hosted by a mutual acquaintance. He showed up that night dressed in a makeshift Nixon costume, while she arrived all decked out in pre-Victorian finery, like some snobbish Jane Austen heroine. Despite the dim lighting and the four drinks he'd downed, he recognized her, recalling a spat they'd gotten into at the newspaper meeting over the aptness of a certain metaphor. He'd found her curiously attractive, intelligent, maybe a little too self-assured —different from the other girls he'd known. Oh, hi, he said as he pulled back his mask and revealed a pair of flushed cheeks. Then, feeling compelled to say something more when she didn't reply, who are you supposed to be?

The next day, Brian remembered, he awoke groggy and cotton-mouthed, legs tangled in unfamiliar silky sheets, with a giant *Les Misérables* poster looming above him. He felt a bit unsteady as he dragged himself from the strange bed, and at the sight of Melissa padding out of the nearby kitchenette, wrapped in a red kimono, a blast of nausea hit him. When she noticed him astir, she moved to her desk, poured a cup of coffee from a French press—an appliance he'd never seen before—and brought the drink to him without saying a word. He recoiled slightly as he accepted the chipped porcelain mug—back then, he didn't really like coffee, at least not without heaps of cream and sugar—but, wanting to avoid any unpleasantness, gulped down its murky contents anyway. The awkward conversation he'd expected, and hoped to avoid, came later.

Despite their differences, their oft-torrid arguments, Brian and Melissa stayed together until graduation. Afterward, he landed a job in Washington, and for a few years, they cohabited there, him churning out copy for a metro daily, her trying to pen a novel. But they drank too much, fought too often, and finally, declaring she'd had enough of that insular little town, of him, she fled to New York. He pursued her, making the trip to see her whenever he could, desperate to win back her favor. And things went on that way through most of their twenties, him lunging, her parrying, until one day she decided to quit the bout. During their last conversation, a maudlin phone call on New Year's Eve, she lamented having to accept a lowly copyediting position at some unglamorous outpost in Hoboken. Just until her book sold, she vowed to him, though the tension in her voice belied her professed conviction. Later, he heard she'd hooked up with one of her former professors, cajoled him into marrying her, and traded her manic life in the city for a quiet one upstate.

Brian glanced down at the picture again and let out a protracted sigh. He had Melissa's number buried in a drawer somewhere, he knew. And for a long while, he thought about searching for it, calling her, asking her about the photo, about things, but then reconsidered. Besides, he mused, this picture, this lone, sad snapshot of her, probably said it all.

America's Roadkill Survivor

Uncle, old-world innocence
marked your foreignness as noticeably
as the Joseph Stalin mustache.
Always eager to share, you offered
two greedy drifters a ride
in your shiny new Plymouth.

When they pulled you from
behind the driver's wheel
and demanded your wallet,
disbelief probably clouded your eyes.

You dropped your car keys
deep into your clothing,
thought only of protecting
your American status.
Infuriated, those thieves took it all,
beating you senseless.

Dragging the naked wreckage
of your broken body down the street
to a neighboring farmhouse,
I wonder if you realized
America wore the unpolished oxfords
that kicked in your ribs,
left you bleeding by the roadside
to die, disenfranchised.

Communion Portrait

They stand, one line above the other,
stern Italian matriarchs in black suits,
three devout Catholic daughters.
The girls wear white veils and pale satin dresses,
hands virginal and folded as trained,
into prayer position.

Their stoic mothers are pushing them
toward the abyss of first Holy Communion,
wishing them a fantasy world of unsoiled saints,
lives devoid of unpaid bills and hard-drinking husbands,
messy childbirth or messier miscarriages,
priests who insist they obey and obey.

Each feels the hand of another dead woman
impatiently pressing her shoulder
as they repeat generation after generation
of strict Church tradition,
believing the continued sacrifice
of their own flesh and blood
will redeem the poor choices each made
to leave innocent childhood.

JENNIFER LAGIER

Sleeping with the Cat

Hunger worms its way
beneath my skin
to unscratchable depths.

From night's lonely corners,
ghosts of men I have loved
come to circle my bed.

Unwanted and alone,
I cling to chilly pillows,
put my hands on myself.

Outside, a swollen moon hangs
above turgid squash,
miles of gaping gold blooms.

Bottle Tree, 1831

after Frankie Silver

They say it's sunlight
that kills them—

spirits caged
inside blue glass

the evil in them
dazzled by beauty,

burnt beyond seeing.
Early morning.

Sheets flapping
on the line,

the baby asleep
in her crib, breath

wrapped snug
in a dream,

the day soft,
soft. Last night's

storm—bruise of
clouds, split lip sky—

gone, gone,
all the violence

siphoned into eternity
like water

funneling
down a drain.

On the other side
of screen door

wind traces its fingertips
over gaps in

silence, sings
lullabies to God.

LORI LAMOTHE

Little Risks

The glass delusion is an extraordinary psychiatric phenomenon
in which people believe themselves to be made of glass.
—Victoria Shepherd

A man whose mind may break
requests asylum
in a padded room.
He fears the ire of chairs
and table edges,
floors so slick with wax
they shine puddles and shattered mirrors.
He fears the women in white
who float unseen around corners,
all elbows and invisible angles.

At night his dreams pace corridors.
His body still, still,
      his breath a wind battened down,
his bones shuttered and the world
turned interior.

This morning I stepped out the front
door, slid a key into ignition
and waited for routine
to scatter the usual sparks across gasoline—
everyday a letter read so many times
life's worn down to
                translucence.
In parking lots daylight falls and goes on
                      falling
through me, burns holes in my shadow.

LORI LAMOTHE

X-Ray

Small bones,
the technician
tells me, coaxing
a curve of spine
into place, *like*
photographing
a blade of grass.
I wonder where
she is, this ghost
of a girl—all frailty
and spirit—locked
inside my body's
cage. I want
to pin her picture
up against light,
study the map
of her skeleton
and chart a path
to the heart
of strangeness.
When I get there
I'll lay my palms
across her back
and reach until I
feel the filaments
of wings, the unseen
architecture of song,
thrashing under my
grip—mad to break
the hold of such
ordinary hands.

Surfing YouTube on September 2nd

And I know a drifter when I see one.
She is a drifter. Her backpack is made
Of rainbow tiger skin. The crickets stun
Up a rhythm and a background for glade
Improvisation. The green man and fun

Lizard woman watch moving pictures of
Beef guys cuddling kittens. Far off there is
A forest where a girl showers in a
Waterfall. The light settles on the trees.
The eyes of iguanas blink sleepily.

One guy has his head gripped tight in the fist
Of a giant his woman can't resist.
It is evening and water cascades higher
Into darkness. It is too wet for fire.

SEAN LAUSE

Deer-Haunted through the Alice Woods

Deer-haunted through the Alice woods,
love is the all-embrace of silence.
Whispers seek where wisdom hides,
and a child escapes the wound of names,
and need not fear a ruinous Queen.
Deer-haunted through the Alice woods,
secrets from a magical mirror
tell a fawn's reprieve from fear,
where a single word spells time's return
and the end of Summer's dream.
Deer-haunted through the Alice woods,
no judgments, for now, may enter,
no writing desk, no raven, no need
to change the subject, a haven
where Alice rules the knights of innocence.
Deep within bewildered trees,
neither here nor there, we are one
as prisoners are one in darkness, till
the King wakes, and we are alone again,
deer-haunted through the Alice woods.

Concertos in the Living Room

me, classical music,
listening to Mozart,
you, painting concertos

—

a violin gushes through
your/their concert
music takes on a disparate note
makes its mock triumphant

—

God is in the living room
his face comes through
the study in fluorescent tones

—

we were frolicking
near the carpeted silks
of red, green and blue,
spinning Arachne's web
little children in
the crisp azure of a dance.

ELEANOR LEVINE

Grandma in the Trailer Park

Grandma grew up
in a Newark high rise
where people borrowed
cottage cheese and eggs

at 82 she was
kicked out of an apartment
because Orthodox Jews were
building a *shul*
and kosher butcher shop
no room for her soap
operas and hamburgers
frying in water

in Jackson, NJ, we
put Grandma in a trailer
the size of a studio
with a lady named Trinity
who believed in Jesus but didn't
preach to Grandma who
couldn't walk well and had
difficulty getting to religious services

Grandma ate gefilte fish along the Formica
counter where Mickey Rourke
spilled beer in *The Wrestler*

the steps weren't high
the bed was near the bathroom
by the kitchen
with toast burning
and *Jeopardy* playing on TV

Who's There

WHEN WE MAKE our night drives, Mom lets me sit up front. When it's not the middle of the night, she wants me in the back, buckled in. But for this she needs me next to her. Every now and then, she grabs my leg. She doesn't look at me. The gesture is so quick, sometimes I think I imagined it.

Three hours after I went to bed, she gently nudges me from sleep.

"Sebastian. I'm sorry. We need to go. Real quick."

She hurries from the room to gather her keys. Her shoes. Her coat. I pull my jeans from the floor and slip them on, stiff and cold from the floor. I glance back at the bed. I know we'll be back soon.

My mom's car glides across town. The roads are empty in our neighborhood. Silent houses pass by the window, cookie-cuttered in rows.

As we move onto the highway, the street lights bounce off the windshield and I watch the transition from light to dark, light to dark, light to dark across the dashboard of our car.

The air is thick, heavy. Mom hasn't said a word since she woke me up.

"Are you sure Dad's there?"

She nods.

"Do I have to go to the door?"

"We'll just wait and see."

We pull in the drive. Tires crunch on rocks. In the quiet, every sound shatters.

Mom sighs.

The porch light is on.

That means I need to go up.

"I guess I'll be right back," I say. I wait a beat. She stares straight ahead. She's trying to smile for my sake. *This is normal. This is okay.* I can feel the words running through her mind.

I nod for no particular reason and open the car door.

I reach the front door of the house, and my gut churns. I knock and wait. I know who will come to the door. It won't be my dad.

Jane cracks the door and peeks. A sly grin spreads her red, glossed lips. Her bright nails click on the edge of the door. Her voice is near a laugh. "Hey there, Sebaaaaastian." I hate the way she says it. "Whoops! Time's up, I guess, darlin'. Hold on," she purrs.

I choke down the bitter taste rising in my throat.

She leans back from the door and into her house, and I hear her call my dad's name.

"Da-an!" Extra As in his name too. "Guess who's here." She laughs and sways, hanging onto the door. Her shiny robe barely reaches her knees. The fabric belt dangles down her legs and I stare at it, willing it to close. She makes a few steps toward the porch and I move out of her path. Her eyes search for my mom in the car, but all I can see is the back of Mom's head. She won't look this way. She never looks when I'm at the door. Jane's hand reaches out to stroke my hair, but I twist my head and look at the ground.

"She ain't all there, huh?" Her head jerks toward the car. "I mean why else would she keep at it? I know she's your mama, but she's just not all there, right?"

I memorize the cracks in the cement of her porch and shrug.

"She knows. Hell, half the town knows. She knows, but she doesn't do a damn thing about it. And then she makes you do the dirty work? While she just sits and waits? It's just not right. You know, if she were a better wife, he wouldn't do this. You know that, right? That's why I'm sayin', there's gotta be somethin' not all *there* with her. Something off or whatever?"

All her sentences sound like questions, but she doesn't wait for answers.

She's talking to me more than anyone's talked to me all week, and part of me wants to say something back. Part of me wants to empty out all the thoughts in my head and try out an adult conversation to see how it fits. But, no. I don't want to talk to her. I really don't want to talk to anyone.

Every day, I sit alone at lunch at school. I hate sitting in silence in the loud hum of the cafeteria. Everyone else sits and talks and trades food. But not me. I do wish, though, that I could sit alone on the bus. But my neighborhood is full of bus kids, so there's always two, maybe three, to a seat. Some days, I sit on the floor in the aisle, hoping the bus driver doesn't see me in the rearview mirror. It's just easier to stay down when one of the other kids has pushed me there.

I don't mention any of this at home. I don't tell my mom about the way kids sometimes throw scraps of paper in my hair. And I never tell her about the way my teachers look at me—like I'm caught behind glass and they just want to let me out. When they see that I've noticed them looking, their lips go thin and their eyes scurry another direction. It's only nice to watch something trapped when it doesn't see you watching.

My nails are digging into the palm of my hands. I stretch out my fingers and stare at the half-moon creases dug into my skin. I feel the blood pulsing just beneath the surface.

I think of how my mom used to kiss me good-night. How my dad used to read me books before bed, his hand resting on my head, his bottomless voice vibrating my bed. Back before the union contract was up. Back before he spat at my mom about filthy scabs and not giving a shit what her father thought he should do. I think of how mom used to yell and scream and tear things from the wall. Curtains off hooks, pictures off the wall, all of it mounded in the middle of the floor for me to find come morning. The heat of her anger would travel down the hall and suffocate me in my room. Later, in the night, she'd come to my bed, crying and apologizing for what I had to hear. But at some point along the line, the fights cooled, like somebody opened a window and let all the energy out. My mom stopped yelling and started nodding, biting her lip, and wringing her hands. Everything in the house felt empty, like if anybody moved too much, the roof might not stay up. I couldn't decide if the before or the after was closer to normal. I couldn't decide what I wanted them to be.

My dad's heavy footfalls stomp down the stairs inside. The door opens wide as he leans back and groans. His thick breath cuts through the night air. He takes a swig from his can, crunches it between his fingers, and drops it near a box by the door. His belch reverberates against the porch's metal awning and the hairs on the back of my neck stiffen.

"Well, Jane, hon', guess I got to go—my chariot awaits." He gives a sweeping bow and laughs but the sound is hard. It is rough on my ears.

I turn my head as he leans to kiss her. I hope his lips find her cheek, the top of her head, the back of a hand, but I can hear the sound of his mouth on hers.

I think of the way Ms. Dungo, the school janitor, and I had to fish my clothes out of the dumpster behind the school last week. How the rain had filled the bottom with sludge and I'd climbed inside to fish out my sweater and jeans. How when she and I'd walked back into the school, a group of kids made kiss noises behind my back. I'd spent the rest of the day in my gym uniform, goosebumps pebbling my arms and legs while I kept my eyes on the floor or my desk.

As I heard my dad's lips linger on Jane's mouth, a giggle in her throat at our family's expense, my shoulders tightened and I squeezed my eyes shut. I turned my head toward the driveway and willed it to be empty. For Mom to have backed the car out silently, turned down the street and driven away. Away from all this, even if she'd left me behind.

But when I open my eyes they lock with hers. She's turned her head this way for the first time. The hard line of her lips pinch and they almost disappear. She nods tightly, and in the space from her to me, I feel the weight of her shame.

Cane-Bottom Chairs

A howling wind
swirls leaves toward the gully,
and fire wood is stacked
by a cabin's back door.
Snow falls in the valley
and on the mountaintop.
Roads soon become ice-paths
that keep neighbors away.

Shade from the mountain
preserves patches of snow
in off-road ditches through
late April. In May, white
oaks shade an old man, as he
shores up the cabin's porch,
its fallen railing, and his wife,
as she mends cane-bottom chairs.

Gateway

With this headache,
I imagine God speaking softly

yet hot & direct like a hair dryer
held too close to the neck.

Gray clouds buffer actual reply
to my thought-scattered prayer.

Piercing neck-pain brings me
an avalanche: churning dirt, jagged

stone. I chew orange clods of muddy
clay, as sun departs in soft purple.

Then: *Step out toward the impending
fire that will—in time—negate the*

*romance of your dreams, where
azalea bushes are floral hillocks*

*beside the cabin door, toadstools
pop up by the pink yard flamingoes.*

Dare I trust the voice of silence,
spoken during my soul-darkness?

The Devil's Fifth Horse

I LOST MY DAD at one of those crazy used-car/used-musical-instrument dealerships. This was years back when they were so popular. Half of everybody we knew strolled around the showroom checking out the deals: a Corvette and an upright piano, a Toyota and a tuba on a stand, a Ford F150 with a set of drums in the bed.

Daddy laid hands on all the guitars until he found a white one that made him want to sing again. It was an electric Gibson Explorer, shaped like flames, and it had two necks like the god of rockabilly designed it himself. It was beautiful.

He probably wanted to dance, too, except Daddy had given up dancing after that time Momma caught him laying hands on Aunt June down at the Tic Toc Club. Momma ran him down with her Dodge Dart, which was too small to outright kill him but plenty big enough to give him a permanent limp.

After that night, Daddy wouldn't ride in the Dart again—he called it the Devil's Fifth Horse—but he stayed at home with Momma on Saturday nights, and if he wasn't happy, he pretended he was.

Then, the Dart stalled out on a set of railroad tracks. Momma fiddled with the ignition until the last possible second. She prayed the train would stop, and the engineer —though he blew that long warning whistle—prayed the car would drive. He pulled the brakes too late, and by the time he stopped, Momma's Dart was squeezed between the locomotive and the crossing sign's flashing red lights. The Dart's frame was twisted like a Judas tree.

"Just desserts for the devil's fifth horse," Daddy said. Sometimes when he said it, I wasn't sure if he meant the car or Momma.

It was Momma who sent us to buy a new car to replace the Dart, but it was Daddy who said the used-car/used-musical-instrument dealer had the best bargains. She told me to keep an eye on him, but I never saw the harm in Daddy looking at the guitars. I missed his music in the house and in our lives. I missed him being wild and reckless. Also, I guess I was as blind as everybody else who doesn't see a man with a pronounced limp as a flight risk.

Just before he disappeared, we were both trying to escape all of the people we knew who were also in need of music and transportation. We had successfully evaded two of Daddy's second cousins, Momma's Sunday School teacher, and a girl I kissed once way back in the second grade.

It was also then that I got absorbed in a demonstration of an old-timey lyre. I couldn't play it and never intended to learn, but I found myself offering the salesman thirty-five dollars for it. That son of a bitch smiled like a cat that flossed with feathers, and I knew I'd been had, but I didn't care. I liked the way that lyre looked.

It wasn't until after I paid the man that I discovered Daddy had made his own deal for the guitar and a 1956 Chevy truck, which he wasted no time in pointing to the road. He didn't tell me goodbye, and he didn't come home again for two years. When he did come, it was on foot and without that two-necked Gibson. Without a dollar in his wallet, either.

We were so happy to see him upright and back in the same country that we were shocked when Momma asked how he lost his limp. Everyone was happy, I should say, except Momma.

RICHARD LUFTIG

Traveling through Illinois

God must have been a farmer
or at least afraid of heights.
Only that can explain this
land so flat, so plumb
that you'd be able to see clear

to forever or Missouri,
whichever came first if it wasn't
for the horizon of corn that makes
a valley of this county road
and swallows up your car.

But if you would only get out
and walk these fields for a while,
out beyond the knotted tree-
breaks, bend down, touch
your palm to the earth, you would

feel where topography resides,
among contours of ghosts
traveling through on their way
to somewhere else, but some still
settling for what this land had to yield,

now eroded, worn smooth
by their stories, each life,
each nearly abandoned
town strung with remembrances
like small dots on a map.

VERONICA LUPINACCI

Independence Day

From the rooftop of an apartment building
I watched my heart explode in a dahlia shock

above the city. The resounding bomb of God
popping a bottle of champagne.

We laid beneath on sheets of bubble wrap
and laughed, like children, at our tiny eruptions.

Then the bridge shook its head
and pieces of me fell like salt onto the river—

dissolving in lithium red petal rain.
Not like paint,
but like blood in water.

Clouds dripped down the ink edge
of the moon and midnight blue matte strokes cracked
a draped canvas sky.

Come sit with me here
and we can dangle our legs through the rails
like we are prisoners of the edge of the roof—

swinging our feet,
swilling silver booze,
clanking a cheer, and spitting stars

on the sidewalk below.
The gravel will imprint on the backs of our thighs
and behind our knees, we will be a little red forever.

How to Pray

Believe in the stitching that binds day to night, however frayed
or fine the days themselves might be. Believe in breath, in words,
in fire and wood and all that has come out of their joining.
Believe in dark, the great unseen half of our lives, in the shining

tack heads of stars holding up ragged tapestries of night.
Believe in the moon that keeps it secrets better than ours.
Believe in the breath, the body, two things we can control
down here where it's hard to believe. Believe that I believe.

One Reason Horses Are Immortal

I can't help believing the horses I saw run
beside the wire fence that wrapped the pasture
auditioned for the role of fire or shadows,
something visible but impossible to catch.

                                    When
I was a boy, I played on the sloped sides of burial mounds
built by a tribe that no longer exists. I didn't know how
to phrase it, but a bit of sky flowered in my chest
when I was out there. One summer, archaeologists dug
trenches, opened the ground to cracked
and time-browned skeletons we had walked over
for years.

            The longer we looked at them, the less
we could explain their presence. Driving home, we passed
a field of horses restless as river current, cousins
to the horses I saw this morning, muscles sliding
endless as tides under sun burnished skins,
like the little bones in my chest sliding open to let
the sky nest there, where dreams run
into fields, where silence keeps us awake.

Cheap Ornithologist at the Séance of Birds

I am not quite convinced the radiance
of cardinals outside the window portends the dead.

The man you wanted to conjure was not in this room: the psychic's pendant
never moved when she called his name. Salt

spilt across the animal cards she spread. The owl
upside down, the owl upside down, and again, upside down:

a wisdom meaning deceit. And then what? I'm not convinced
you taped the photo he took of the omniscience

of godwits along the shore secure enough
to the wall. Unglued from the spackle, it swooped down

on the heat from the vent. All ghosts
and predators stayed away. My disbelief propped

up with a broom through its back, scarecrow in the cornfield. I apologize
for frightening the birds: even the murder, the prey of hawks.

Renewal

Dusk fall and I'm standing on the sixth floor of the parking garage
where last night a young man, 26, jumped for reasons unexplained.

From this distance, the plaza looks artificial, almost
as if the people below are being inserted into place

with a toothpick, the space between ground
and railing encapsulated and filled with music, the model set in a toy store.

Leaning over the railing, my elbows dip like oars into the invisible
current. I crane my neck upwards to observe the stars

fighting to make their presence felt like supporting actors
in a play of streetlights.

Like a fairy tale, the air feels heavy with promise and I imagine
jumping into a jet stream like a vagrant hopping a train car,

the country fleeting and invisible until first warm light
breaks over the landscape, giving voice to the muted trees.

Suddenly, I'm no longer on the sixth floor of the parking garage
but flying over a dominion of renewal where even the ruins

decompose into nutrients like leaves finding purpose after death.
Like acorns breaking out of their wet tombs after falling into earth,

growing strong under the fertile soil, becoming in old age
something beautiful and wise.

JOSHUA LEE MARTIN

Sunday Alms

Bare-backed under an unforgiving Mississippi sun,
my father pauses his dance with the shovel, rests
a lick while mosquitos rise from the lake to stake

out plots of red flesh to savor. We watch him
through the bay window, let tears soak through sleeves
of Sunday bests as he resumes his work heaving

clods into the magnolia-blossomed air. Later he'd say
he never saw the golden retriever unfurl herself slowly
like the sinews of an unused muscle behind the rear-axle

of our truck, never heard a whimper or low-baritone
last bark as he edged into reverse, but in that moment
all he wants is to be left alone to wrap his burden

in a shroud of towels, to lower his guilt to a point
just above the water-table.
I remember the only alms offered to him

coming at nightfall: the cool cotton shirt pulled
taut over his pockmarked shoulders, and my
mother's voice at dinner, soothing as a church hymn,
still singing something of his goodness.

The Way Things Are

No matter the length of prayer to Mary or Vishnu
the hungry beagle, if left alone, will take

the chicken in its mouth *every time* to renounce
the fable of harmless predator and savvy prey.

It will wait until you are inside, asleep or stupefied,
before marching around the coop like Joshua at Jericho,

its trumpet the bark of instinct, looking for gaps
in the woodwork weakened by muzzle's prodding.

How quickly the predator's brain commands
its body's singular purpose, its yellow

eyes pulsating with desire, its fangs unsheathed
like slivers of moon knifing through cloud cover,

zeroing the carotid. Then, the chicken's abrupt shrill
and your daughter's jolting out of bed.

In the morning, you'll chain the dog to the kennel,
saying, *honey, that's just how life is*

before sniffing out the last of the unbroken eggs
buried deep in the flaxen straw.

Then, you'll grease up the griddle.
Then, you'll beg her to eat.

JO McCREARY

Covenant

Stark white egret under the moon,
claws clasped to its nest.
Rides the swift Savannah River
out of its hemorrhaging refuge.
Legs erect. Head held high
against the tidewater wind.

With a man made strange by marriage,
the woman sits on a deck
at a white-clothed table.
River dredged and waterfront piled
just beyond.
Smell of death and new excavation.

Her fingers, on the stem of a glass,
pickaxed by candlelight.

Towel draped over his forearm,
the waiter pours red wine.
As the rigid white neck first appears
around a bend.
Eyes terrified, round and black
on either side of its head, dead-eyeing the current.
Deadly, holy channels of water.
Wine swirls up the woman's glass.

MATT McGEE

The Contributing Author

THE LATEST EDITION from the Illinois publisher arrived on a warm February day in LA. The book had been sent in a thin, brown cardboard box, taped with weight-appropriate packing tape and, as the opening revealed, wrapped in the kind of blue tissue paper that tops off a perfect holiday gift. Probably, I thought, a leftover lying around the publisher's home.

I leaned into a secondhand wingback chair, five feet from where my father occupied its sagging twin. There in the breezeway his wife has allowed him to decorate with remnants of our past life; family photographs taped up, a couple paintings dabbed when he was about my age, hung now on bare frame walls. There isn't even drywall to nail into; you just hammer directly into a stud, hang your picture and Home Sweet Home. This life is an agreement made through the church decades earlier.

I unwrapped the book from its magical blue tissue. Dad made the kind of confused face that's been coming on a couple years now. Doctors say it's a normal part of the process.

"I've heard that's good," he says.

"Have you read it?"

"No, no. But I've heard it's good."

I flipped open the table of contents, always the first thing done with an anthology. And there on page 121 in the 300-page book is the name. The words appear just as crafted and the story, about the lament of never becoming a father, has a simplicity and truth I'd forgotten. Storytelling has become like a breadcrumb trail. I handed Dad the book.

He tilted the glasses on his nose. In the silence of his focus I looked out the window at the mailbox; I've given this address to the publishers on purpose. It's not just to avoid the junk mailers.

For years he tucked us in at night. Then he would turn, lift his typewriter off the hallway desk like a fourth child and carry it downstairs to tap into the early hours. The rejection letters bore some of the best names in the business.

He finished with a grunt. "I don't think I get it." I know the contemporary reference to birth control and pregnancy tests are a little past his time. And just as I was about to save him from it, his wife opened the breezeway door.

"It's about time to go, don't you think?"

The confused man stood quickly, already dressed for Mass, and handed the book back to the contributing author. At home I'll set it on the shelf among the others, and someday soon, I'll have to start giving out my real address.

Coda

To speak about the love of your life,
you may need some space,
the distance of bus rides and bar stools,
Cuban postmarks and perhaps the past tense.

The way dark curls softened her shoulder blade,
and the pearl in her left ear.
A tiny dent in her forehead,
the warmth and whispers that for a while
spared you.

ELIZABETH McMUNN-TETANGCO

Bats

The bats
lace like shy fingers

overhead, but
this is marriage, after

all. You wake him up.

You pull
the covers to your chin
watching them

fly; you hold

his arm.

The bats are flecks of ash;
you are the fire—

if there was fire—

hot and shaking
in the bed
in the hotel. What

does it mean, if there are bats in a hotel? You
are afraid. Are they trapped? Later on
you read

the bats are getting sick, that
they are dying, and nobody

can say why. There are pictures
of a bat, in a blank cave, with his eyes
shut. Somebody stood there, taking pictures,
while he slept.

Your husband leaves, but
you can only dream

of bats: their faces close
and their mouths open.

When you drive, after that, you look for them

in the thin sky
but never see them.

Coyotes

Coyotes on the hill
across the lake

are scattered stones. Sharp
high barks. You listen

lying flat, awake
in the old tent. (It was your
father's: thin

and gray as a weak
lung.

My escape

he said, packing on a Friday, kneeling hard
on the lean fabric
to force out unwanted

air.) Your breath

catches
on the nylon; makes
it cry.

You wonder if your father lay here
all alone, with the

limp pulse
of the water in his ears like a reminder.

Did he think about coyotes

about children

with their smiles
and vacant eyes

just across town?

"Why You Holdin' My Hand?"

HE SAW ONLY the white bubbles when he looked at Greg's chin. The innocence of those bathtub whiskers faded and were replaced by proper hairs. Long and stringent and frayed and born from years. Greg's cold, chapped hands rested in his own and the calluses they bore together, the homes they built that they would never reside in, echoed in the foundations of those hard areas. The theme from *All in the Family* came through the speakers of the television and called Greg back from sleep. His cobalt eyes gazed at similar features still full of life staring back at him from in front of the stale ceiling lights.

"Why you holdin' my hand, Orin?" The words rode his whisper.

The faint grip scraped those hard spots against Orin's palm like the words from Greg's mouth.

"Your hands is my hands."

"You ain't queer, are ya?"

Orin smiled.

A retched cough erupted behind the curtain. A familiar soundtrack prompting neither to look. Greg yawned and his white lips pulled and stretched enough so that Orin thought he heard the flesh tear.

"You need a drink?" Orin asked.

"I need something."

A clear cup sat on the sterile nightstand and he tipped the cup into those parched lips. The hope of satiation snuffed by the violence of his body's rebellion. Water sprayed skyward, dousing Orin's face but no sheet or towel or shirt reached his skin. He stood on the patchy lawn, the limp hose running from his hand. Mouthful after mouthful, Greg filled the cavern of his mouth and sprayed cool water over Orin till he boiled over in rage and comedy and they took to the ground.

"Won't be long now," Greg said, eyes closed and sunken.

Droplets fell from his chin onto the sheets where bodies became ghosts. Archie Bunker's gruff voice recalled the duel punishments and the belt that dangled from the old man's fist. Greg's stolid eyes never wavered from Orin's bent over the side of the bed.

"Why you holdin' my hand, Orin?"

Their mother always told them to hold hands when they crossed the street. Orin took Greg's lead, held his hand and followed when safe, clear of danger of death, until they crossed the black sea of asphalt like Moses. The grip from Greg's man-sized hands vise-like.

"It's my turn now," Orin replied.

The cobalt eyes half-shuttered now. Their hands together at rest atop Greg's shallow chest. Through that hand, Orin thought he felt whatever was left inside his brother being devoured. The click of a clock perhaps. His eyes stayed on Greg's chest and watched the rise and fall and how much longer between the breaths came.

"Why you holdin' my hand, Orin?"

The fragility of the words almost consumed by his breath. A tear crept from the corner of Greg's eye and slid down his waxen cheek. His skin the same color from that time they stole Dad's cigarettes and smoked for the first time. A faint squeeze pressed his hand and Greg's eyes forever shuttered. Orin stared at their entwined hands and stood on the other side of that black sea. A vise-like grip for Greg.

KEN MEISEL

Our Lady of the Rosary

Bring her in I say. It is nearing rush hour
and the sunset along Woodward Avenue
melts into nasturtium yellow down I-94.
I have been drinking at a lonesome bar
where a Vietnam veteran, searching
for porn on a small computer, has broken
into chrysanthemum tears over the loveliness
of a woman's thighs. I have left there
and walked up into this church to silence
my mind of rumination and trouble.
And so the priest brings her in. She seats
herself in a swarm of light that resembles
flowering kale and swimming mackerel.
The light funnels through the rose window.
A small fly trying to escape tortures itself
against glass. The priest hands me a black rosary.
We begin with the Sorrowful Mysteries.
It is not what I expect. She tells me this is for
the end of your life. Asks me what I have done
with Desire. I answer it is a fish I have chased.
Asks me should I ever catch it. I answer
it is not catchable. Mackerel swarm around
the shape of her body. My hands quiver.
Become fish. She asks if I have committed
Avarice. I answer the shape of a woman
has changed the way my eyes see and so yes.
I say that Avarice is just the confusion
of the flesh against the Ineffable, and so yes.
I have committed Avarice all my life.
I have chased the shape of a woman
through my pupils all of my life. Yes. I've
confused her with the Ineffable falling apart.
The priest moves nervously in his seat.

She asks me to speak of the Crucifixion.
It is the hill on which the Ineffable
and Avarice pray, I say. And we spend
our youth running into it, confusing it
with suffering, with clinical depression,
with all manner of pharmaceutical remedy.
The halo of thorns has hummingbirds
surrounding the head. They are sins.
Also they are the prayers we pray ecstatically.
In the end they are the Holy Spirit in us.
The wood of the cross is the skeleton.
The storm on the hill is substance into spirit.
The hummingbirds are the marvelous,
which is why Avarice and the Ineffable
are the beads we pray along the body rosary.
We pray inside Avarice and Ineffability.
Confuse it with joy, with our suffering.
She waves her hand at me. She stirs
the fish through her silver luminosity
so that they resemble aubergine petals.
Tells me the Ineffable is the holy smoke
inside loving. Breathe it in to yourself.

These Days

I get up early in the morning these days,
listen to the last persistence of crickets

rubbing the stars between their legs
underneath the bushes in the park.

Squat low to the window ledge and listen
to the laughing sound of my one child

playing on the swing in the park all those years
ago when she wore her hair long to her waist

and I brought a plate of peanut butter cookies
out to the monkey bars for all the girls to eat.

I hear the girls laughing until a bird in a tree
shrieks the first ribbon of morning here.

Press my ear against the screen to hear her
boarding the train, falling tired against the seat.

Open the book she is reading as she bites
the apple and sighs the last of her day out.

I imagine her feeling her heartsong until her eyes
close and she is slumped and dreaming a dream

that has a painting of a rainbow parading
over the gray buildings of San Francisco Bay—

as the morning fog rolls into the homes there—
and she blesses herself into her thirtieth year.

Watch her as she leaves the ceramics studio,
pottery in hand, to offer the world her gift.

Tip my ear for the night hawk's final
feverish yelp as the evening's black clot

is slowly torn open into the gray morning—
and the roadside around me fills with cars.

Clown Cars

IN THE MANUFACTURING process everything depends on the trap door. I'm the one who hangs them on their hinges. Without me, a carload of clowns tops out at five or six.

People expect surprises. We crave seeing impossible things, as in *man oh man, those clowns sure keep spilling out!* Put about four clowns in a car and wait for bankruptcy to catch up; it will. Your circus, your decision.

How I got this spot on the line—and I laugh when I say this so folks can relax—I killed a guy and took his place. People think that's droll. Sure you did, they say. He was only a year older than me, decades 'til retirement. You try being stuck in spot-weld purgatory. Welding. I had a pipe wrench when I passed him in the stairwell. Almost couldn't finish the deed because he begged me to stop.

I was nauseous for a week but didn't call in.

Now I'm the main difference between a Clown Car and a Town Car.

When you're at a circus and they spill out, floppy shoe after red nose, see what you realize about Life. See if a big epiphany comes. It's entirely possible.

We're essentially craftsmen here, making art of vehicles. We only build a dozen cars a shift, but retired clowns on Social Security constantly drive finished ones out of the plant, back in, out again. The casual observer would believe we have an unlimited supply.

Surprise!

Others on the line would do anything to steal this spot. If they come for me, I'm diving down a hole in the employee lot. There's a hinged door in the asphalt. There's a place under there where excess clowns wait to make appearances. They sit packed tight beneath floorboards, just waiting for the signal to amaze.

Chthonic Tom

"...trailing clouds of glory..."
—Wordsworth

THOMAS BYRON has reached a new and higher level I can only know vicariously in his presence. Perhaps he is merely semi-divine. A society will one day be formed in his honor. This morning, Thomas is having coffee and beignets in the courtyard of the Café du Monde. He remembers when the coffee shop opened in 1862. Mr. Bones is also at table.

"I can smell the sea on a northerly breeze," says Thomas, "how wonderful."

"It is only one hundred or so miles south," says Bones, "across delta and bayou."

Thomas is in white except for a black Kentucky string tie. His white fedora rests in an empty chair. Bones, a hyperdimensional being, is a bleach-boned skeleton in tie, tails and top hat. He wears a monocle. He is visible only to Thomas, children of about three years or less, and a homeless man with high brain dopamine levels who occupies a seat in the nearby park.

(When I refused to play the scapegoat any longer, my father and siblings had little use for me.)

An exhibit at the nearby Cabildo Museum, large photographically enhanced pictures of the Shroud of Turin, is on display. Our Thomas had a hand in this. He is on the A-list of donors. Thomas has a genetic fluke; his body produces exceeding levels of anti-oxidants, and his mitochondria produce few oxygen-free radicals. Thomas ages almost imperceptibly. This began in his early twenties. His grandparents, parents, brothers, mother and father, wife, children, grandchildren, nieces, nephews, favorite confessors, priests, friends and enemies, and so on are all gone along the way of the dead. He does not believe in reincarnation. He seems to exist at all times in full bloom. He is seriously alone.

Thomas's ongoing present moment is, however, amazing. He is an advocate of self-improvement. He keeps his body fit. He improves his mind and attitude daily through affirmations and reading. He rides along on a gently swelling tide. He has no need for adverse people or circumstances because he does not believe that he can only grow through suffering.

"So you do believe the Shroud of Turin is Jesus' burial cloth?" asks Bones.

"I want to," says Thomas. "The evidence is compelling."

"Well do you? You either do or you do not."

"I know it probably is, but on a heart level I cannot feel it."

Thomas knew a second cousin who was also lifespan gifted. She was actually nearing the end of her days. This did not upset her. She also finally caught passage along the way of the dead.

(Roaches have high levels of the antioxidant superoxide dismutase. They could survive a deadly nuclear war.)

"You've been human," says Thomas. "What do you know about head-level and heart-level knowing?"

"I never thought about it. This emotional knowledge just happens," says Bones.

Over the levee, in the air above the wide and flowing river, the path of a butterfly is altered by a puff of wind. It perseveres and lands on the table of Thomas and Bones.

"This guy used to be a lowly caterpillar," says Bones.

"The life of this butterfly," says Thomas, "the very being of it, bespeaks an inherent ability to remake oneself, to be one thing and then become something altogether different, glorious, in this very life."

Bones nods in the affirmative. The butterfly flutters away.

A woman close by sees Thomas talking to an empty chair. Her toddler son can see Mr. Bones. The woman could have, too, very early in her life.

An outrageous seraph lands in the courtyard, settles itself and makes for the street. It nods at Thomas and Bones. A three-year-old fellow near the door holds up a hand and slaps the angel a high five.

Safety in Numbers

IT'S SO COLD HERE. This English winter evening, the sky now dark. Piles of frozen slush in the area of the bins. I'm sitting in this churchyard and I am counting. Don't know why except to say it grounds me. I know where I am when I'm embedded in a plain of numbers. My safety zone. Otherwise there's chaos everywhere.

There are fifteen flagstones between me and the nearest tree. Fifteen is not a number I'm that happy with so I count again, this time from the railing just behind my head. Seventeen. Better for me. My birthday's the 17th of March. I'm the two fishes swimming. The yin and yang. This night both of them are entirely made of ice.

The flagstones between tree and portico are thirteen; they say that's unlucky for some. But not for me I think. Thirteen added to seventeen comes to thirty and that's a good round number. There's a howling sound as wind blows round the walls of the church. The door is locked in case of vandals. But maybe I'll go sit in the porch. Must be warmer there.

Inside there are three persons. Two are sleeping. One of them stares out from under the rim of his cap with rheumy half-open eyes. All at once he winks at me, though does not smile. This unnerves me so I sit at the furthest end of the stone seat and count the tiles on the porch wall. I want to get the whole of the wall ahead of me done before I nod off but I'm tired; keep losing track.

Snores from the sleepers echo in my ears. Distant bird cries and the whoosh of night-traffic on the nearby road. I try to calculate the number of times I hear them but lose myself to sleep. Come morning I wake and find two of my companions are gone. The one who was staring into the air remains, the same eyes open still. They stare past me. A glazed and frosted look. This time he does not wink. I think this man is dead.

It is early; the church is still closed up. But it's too late for him. None can help him now, can they. I'm troubled by realizing this. I feel very shaken here huddled at the feet of a dead man. So at last I get up and run through the small church garden, calling out. I think of all the many rough sleepers in this city who will have died in the freezing night just past. When I return with helpers I say a prayer for this homeless stranger who has gone.

The porch is shadowed; the sky turning light. I sit on the stone seat all alone now and study the church door; try as hard as I can to add up all the grains there in the wood; count the number of bricks before me in the surrounding wall, the cracks in the domed ceiling above my head. And attempt to restore my inner peace.

DAVID MIHALYOV

Casting Shadows

Sunrise above the cloud line, airplane taking
me away. Turbulence above, winter below.
Overcast skies won't clear until April,
skeletal trees missing the dressing of leaves.

During summer we walked the cobblestones
of old town. A man stood on a box,
haranguing those around him.
He singled me out as we passed.

Look out, mister,
the salvation bus is coming.
Get on board or go to hell.

What does he know about hell?
you asked. He hasn't been married
to you for fifteen years. You flashed
a winning smile, so I took it as a joke.

The plane wobbles, which brings
the fasten seat belt sign.
The head on the man in front of me looks
like a topographical map and I fight

the urge to reach and allow
my fingers to feel the furrows.
I look out the window
and see hills laid bare by strip mining.

The weak sun
moves around the clouds,
searches for something to rest upon
that would cast a shadow.

Finding nothing, it moves on.
Finding nothing, we all move on.

DAVID MIHALYOV

Dropping Anchor

I drop anchor in deep water,
the shore no longer in sight.
This lake, a Great Lake,
while small on a map
seems like an ocean now.

You climb onto the boat's edge,
balancing yourself to the rhythm
of the waves before diving.
I watch as from outstretched hands
to tensed feet you disappear.

I hold my breath until you surface.
You give your head a shake
and wipe wet fingers
across your eyes, shocked
at the coldness.

You take a few strokes and I see
arms, legs, sleek, gliding,
and I know I'm still in love.
I want to call you back, make love,
but you would never be so brazen.

Instead, you motion for me
to join you. I demur,
mindful of limitations,
not trusting myself in waters
whose depths I cannot reach.

DEVON MILLER-DUGGAN

How He Wandered

Because there had to be a God
who knew the scald and task of our blood,
because there had been a daughter, motherless,
because Jephthah rented his own garment and walked
away from forever his own threshold, barefoot in winter,
because even daughters climb mountains,
because bees die for sweetness,
and the oceans for salt,
and the bark of trees dies for bitterness,
because our weight crazes the stones where we stand,
pulls us toward the burning heart,
Jephthah walks, his feet blooded, healing,
blooded, healing, blooded.

Because the daughter died un-named,
every step he takes forever, every weather
tastes like a knife in someone's hand.

Because the knife in Jephthah's hand
becomes its own storm, he walks,
cutting himself over and over.
The knife will not leave his hand,
and his daughter's name will not leave his throat, therefore
honey and milk on the tongues of infants,
so they will know sweetness,
salt on the tongues of infants
so they will know blood.

Because we are made of water
which never dies, is only sullied, and disbands
back into the mountain of the air,
and because water therefore always moves,
because daughters climb mountains
and fathers keep bargains.

The Way Each Night

as you drop towards sleep,

some shard of a dream you had
the night before darts into memory.

How every dream still walks along your grandfather's creek,
among holly and loblollies, where you know

you're the child who never goes into the creek,
no matter how bright the water,

because no one knows what dark
the water's taken from the land it slides through.

How each dream-shard crowds in, bumps shoulders—
off before you can call it back or

name it. The way it fills your skin with wet leaves
or pine resin. How you force yourself to look

at what you've done, and left undone.
How your feet tear the moss.

THOMAS MITCHELL

The Way Summer Ends

By evening, the live oaks
in their twisted architecture,
straddle the hillsides, the wind
weaving their branches,
silent as the movement of an owl in flight,
dark against the eaves,
circling the moon instead of trees.

I strike a match
and a mantle of stars
churns inside the Coleman lantern,
then swings across the lawn
convulsively.

It's hard to be at home in this darkness.

In the sanctuary of my room,
I can almost hear the broken light,
the half-drawn blinds, the slow dust gathering
in the halo of the lamp.

Ennui

Cicadas vie
with the neighbor's lawnmower.

Pollen
congealed bird shit

the residue
of rain after rain.

It's time
I washed the windows

but today like every day
so much effort

that will only need
repeating.

And anyway when they're clean
the sparrows fly straight

into them. How
like a fist

the invisible can be.

Magician Dreams

I slip into the black
tuxedo of sleep
unshackle myself

above a giant tank
of piranha
catch
the bullet
between my teeth
blindfolded
at fifty paces.

My lovely assistant
saws me into halves
the crowd's faith
in illusion
growing more
unshakeable

with each pull
of her bare and slender arms.

For my finale
I will levitate
hover momentarily
like an angel
then vanish
into the nothingness
up my sleeves.

Hoboken Rimbaud

after David Wojnarovich

Saw Rimbaud
hungry for new visions
in his blindfold
on the church shelter bench.
Around him
quiet men layered
in hooded sweatshirts
& Army jackets
in from the park square,
their shopping carts
left at the door
loaded with blankets,
returnable bottles,
maybe a broom
raised like a flag.
One failed all day
to hitchhike to Newark.
Another kicked out
of his mother's hallway
for blacking out
on Night Train.
A third plans to sleep
in the bus yard.
They wear cold weather
like a chronic disease.
They stare at TV
like hundred-year old
Eskimos.

Rimbaud's their saint.
His graffiti transforms piers
into ruined castles;

pterodactyls crash
through the windows.
His waterfront journals
record outlaw desires.
His poetry band
plays *3 Teens Kill 4*
to gas station crowds.
His monkey
carries the Earth
in a wheelbarrow.
His blue skinned boy
races through the forest
with flames trailing
his limbs like a meteor
burning through love.
His formaldehyde jars
hold a congress of snakes.
His collage of Jesus
shooting up junk
put a bounty on his head.
His Molotov cocktail
hand-labeled
for the White House
has yet to be thrown.
In his blindfold
he wastes no time
on secondhand dreams.
Next week he opens
a bank account, the first
anyone's had in years.

Extinction

You think you're something else now because,
from the top bunk, your feet almost touch the
ceiling when you stretch your legs above your
head, straight as a compass needle pointing

northward. But I think you could dance on top
of the world with those legs, spinning around
your axis across the Ganges while balancing on
toes curled to a pointe like the nose of a river dolphin.

I want to tell you those freshwater dolphins swim
blind and on their side through dim waters,
compelled by distant light and echoes of lost sound,
while the whole world unfurls before you now

like a moonflower. Sometimes I think you radiate
as if lit from within like the Painted Desert when
the light is almost gone and the cliffs turn purple and
glow like the inside of a flame, like a dream.

I remember how, long before we divorced, your dad
and I would drive from Phoenix across the Mogollon
Rim to the Grand Canyon and back in a single day,
and every time I could feel the air getting lighter and

colder the further north we'd go and how I'd press my
nose against the glass of the car window to measure our
progress—just like when I was young, about your same
age now, when your legs are almost long enough to

reach the ceiling. I wonder if you feel like you're
holding up the weight of our world on the bottom
of your feet, the way firstborn daughters do, always
wanting everything right.

That's what I want to say when you summon me a half
hour past bedtime to perform your latest act in the
art of growing up. I want to hold your childhood in my
cupped hands and put it in a mason jar with holes in the

lid, using its light to find my way. Instead, I ask how you
got so lovely in only eleven years. You smile and pull
the moon up to your chin like a blanket, like a dream.

The Vision

I'm rinsing dirty cups when I glance outside the
kitchen window—the one facing the patio
flanked by vines with wild tendrils, a copse of

native azaleas, ivy swallowing a shipwrecked
birdbath in the corner—the patio with a crack
running reptile across the cement where the earth

below it sank. This old house. Too many hollow
places, like the gulley beneath the root cellar that
swells with spring groundwater. Or the inside

of the tire swing that fills with rain and turns to rust.
I fear hidden spaces like I do old oaks with heavy
limbs, empty with decay. I wonder what might

happen on our worst day. Then it catches my eye,
a linear flash of light midair, a beam of reflection
floating. I stop and study the air. A breeze lifts a

diaphanous string of silk suspended like a tightrope
across my patio floor with no beginning or end,
just a middle. The light skips across it, center balancing

before shifting into transparency again, an apparition.
I recall the times I've walked into a spider web,
the thing I couldn't see, frantic to escape the

feeling of wool on virgin skin. But for today I am a prophet.
I only see light dancing on silence, the beauty of the peril.

The Human Library

Who can forget the ending of *Fahrenheit 451,*
    campfire tales reworked by Brothers Grimm,

the rhymes to remember, genesis of epochs?

I once got on *Wikipedia* with John and Andy,
    and we wrote outlandish facts about Ayn Rand:

Hitler's lover, school bus driver, Tae Bo instructor.

In nameless crypts all over the world, prisoners
    are tagged and warehoused by the hundreds,

referenced by interrogators to recheck the facts.

The collective storyteller unearths our history
    from shards of arrows, scrolls, and lost kings,

but who is really behind the unmaking of things?

I am addicted to writing with others, creation
    inseparable from friendship, this act a reservoir

that pumps to and from a writer's haunts.

The first books were probably made of skin,
    early dissertations of how much trouble

we were in, a lost pantheon inventing gods.

The Odyssey is whispered in the dark at hostels.
    We change the narrative when it suits us.

Which reads are bound, and which are boundless?

JAMES OWENS

Red Thought within a Gladiolus Blossom

after a photograph by erin wilson

The image is a garden inside the garden.

Eros as shimmer
as blood unfurls
through the wall of this wound
that opens the air like a sex.

The strokes of her looking
breathe
the petals to further opening and opening
and un-
fold
membrane contour texture.
Different wet reds shine.

All this from dirt and sun and water
dust the flower has healed
sepal
ovule
anthers laden dark
nudge of a cell upward
any touch would soft to bursting
and scatter sperm
inside the four chambers of the stone.

An Only Child Tours the Library in Whitesburg, Kentucky

A visitor idly walking the shelves, tired,
wondering who in town served the best coffee,
I came upon
volumes of Kentucky birth statistics bound in black.

What a lark—look myself up, see if I existed.

Then I remembered another.
I'd never seen his name,
never heard if he had one,
never seen a photo.
No one spoke of him
except once Mother said,
"When your baby dies,
they move you out of the ward,
put you in a room by yourself,
don't want you upsetting the other new mothers."

I could stroll on,
still keep forgetting him

May 30, 1948, his birthday

named after our father

his tiny hand waving at me through lines of print.

An August Day in Southern Ohio, 1851

A woman sits in a straight chair
On the porch of a clapboard farmhouse
Breaking an apronful of pole beans
Into a tin wash pan
And looking out on fields where distantly
Under the brass clock of the sun
Her husband is plowing with the mule.
In a cradle at her feet the baby sleeps,
A dark curl sweated to his forehead.
She thinks of that November day last year
When her name was lifted into history
By a census taker recording for the first time
The names of the women and children
Along with Head of Household.
Her age, too, was marked down, eighteen,
And the place she was born,
As if she mattered.
What a wonder, she thinks,
That the government cares who I am!
People I will never see!

Just then,
Though the light does not change,
She feels a shadow pass between her and the sun,
As if a great bird is flying overhead, wings spread,
And a chill rushes through her hair,
As if a breeze is caught in it.
Now she recalls stories
The old residenters tell of the Shawnee
And how in those days, when you got the feeling
Someone was watching,
You paid attention to it.
She picks up the baby and the pan of beans,
Goes inside and shuts the door.

I sit back from my computer
Pausing in my genealogical search
To touch her name on the screen.
She will have eleven more children.
Her husband will be shot in the face at Shiloh
And never be able to work the land again.
She will live to open the door
To four more census takers.
I rub my eyes and wait
For her to edge aside
A window curtain
And peep out.

LEE PASSARELLA

And the Sea Gave Up the Dead

On the raising of Confederate submarine H. L. Hunley,
world's first submarine to sink a military target,
the U.S. Housatonic, February 17, 1864

...the bilge pump couldn't handle
the big sea that swamped us;
we went down as if we'd shipped hot lead
instead of brine. Still, before it was all done,
we had time to think on death,
and on our own misdeeds. Even righteous blood
gloves your hands so they can't feel things
as they ought. That Yankee ship we sundered
with our spar torpedo: Sailors come to trust
their ships as they trust God's covenant
with that Old Mariner in Genesis.

We'd yanked the bluecoats' little world out
from under them. We were their Day of Wrath,
Thief in the Night. In those few moments
I had to think on things before I slept,
I remembered that clever murder,
along with all the little, little crimes
we suppose black our fame in the Book of Life.
After this the judgment, you *may* have heard tell.

But when that long sleep comes, it comes quick.
Oh, it *is* a stunning, break-through-the-ice-
over-head-and-ears type of cold.
Your nose gripes you terribly. Your lungs
scream at you like the sea's made of turpentine.
But you get used to "breathing" your new element
at last. God bathes, then beds you down. Blue or gray....

Knuckle Bear 6

I like snakes, look wet feel dry.
Papaw catch the copperhead
Say it the one kill Blue
Put it in paceboard box
One he fetch grocery in
Tape it with duck tape
Put at end of garden
By dry up squash plants
We sit listen snake hiss
Strike end of box
Then Papaw pour gas
Scratch match against his zipper
Then pow the fire shoot
Taller than the corn stalks
And he say Knuckle Bear
Pay attention for oncet
That how you turn a
Copperhead into a black snake.

Crushing Houses

THE WRECKING BALL hung over the roof. The machine paused seconds before crashing down on the top of the house. The house fell into itself, layer upon layer, over and over again. Lindsey watched mesmerized. By the fifth time the house was crushed, she moved over to another wall of the gallery which held hundreds of photos of rooms, one with just the remains of a wallpapered wall, the blue and gold flowers still intact. A soundtrack blared sirens and lights flashed. She blinked at the assault and covered her ears.

"Who did this?" She asked when Moira came over.

"Damian. Who would have thought?"

"Who?" Lindsey snapped out of her reverie. Moira pointed to a skinny hunched over guy standing alone in the corner.

"Remember him from drawing class?"

Lindsey peered over Moira's shoulder. "Not really. He did this?"

"Pretty intense stuff."

Lindsey walked over to where he was standing. There were two people now around him, but he didn't seem to be making much effort to talk to them; so she said, "Hello. I'm Lindsey. I guess we were in class together. Do you remember?"

He lifted his gaze up from the floor. "Which class?"

"Moira said Drawing. It's ok. I don't remember either. These are incredible, the pictures and the house. I mean, how do you do them?"

"I was in Detroit. They have this thing where artists can stay in a house for free. I had a couple of friends living in one so I did it. They tear down a house every day of the year. Even on Christmas."

"No kidding. That house didn't look so bad."

"It wasn't." They were left alone talking while the other two people were relieved to be able to move on, or at least Lindsey thought so.

"But the fires? All those houses. How do you find them?"

Damian bent his head slightly. "I have a police radio. I drive out when I hear the fire alarm.

"So, you follow the fire trucks?"

"Yeah. It sounds weird, but there's something beautiful in a fire. And then you see the life that's left behind. Nothing could be more personal."

"It's like invading someone's privacy."

"No, it's naked. It's already exposed. It's what's left of life. Debris. Mess, you know."

"And that's the only way to get those pictures?"

"Pretty much. They tear them down pretty fast. This way I know where to find them."

"No fire and flames in the pictures. You almost wouldn't know what happened."

"That would be too obvious."

"I guess." Lindsey wanted to get away without being impolite. "Crushing those houses, why do they do that?"

"That's different. That's speculation. I could live in some of those places they tear down."

Lindsey tried to catch Moira's eye from across the room. "I have to get back to my friend. Congratulations. It's a good show."

Damian shrugged and walked over to the table where wine was being served. Lindsey wanted nothing more than a calming glass of cabernet but didn't want to talk about destruction anymore.

Moira came over and Lindsey spoke. "Why didn't you tell me? He is really weird."

"No weirder than most."

"He listens to a radio to find out where fires are."

"So do reporters."

"Maybe he's really a pyromaniac."

"Maybe. But it is pretty impressive stuff."

"Don't you find it creepy? Just a little?"

"Of course. But people paint with their own blood and embalm sharks. I think this is innocent compared with piss and blood."

Econlockhatchee Song

O shadow figure of Mary's
white statue,
greet us as we come up
the banks at night,
the blackwater
pool of Shady Oaks Trailer Court.

Our ritual is to smack her face
      we're not the least bit sorry
on our tiptoe home through the scrub pine.
We shush cataract-eyed baby possums
and locust trills. Blind swordsmen,
we feel our way through evening-length works
of mosquito song and swamp swims.
We have need of no vision.

Our Man sings his whiskey woe,
switch-whips us when we sneak back in,
finds us wet and muddy.
The saw palmetto scratches
sting less, sing more.
Sing the praise,
pray to our sinners.

Two Old Musicians

These are the men of war
the men of rusted guitar strings
whose lyrics reach like rough chains
from their mouths down their chins
tickling the ankles of their sons
and grandsons, reminding
the young men of old humiliation.
But young feet forget the old rhythms,
and young men's soles are not scarred,
having not walked
the hot sands of their ancestors.
They are soft and seek soft ways
in the shade of the bougainvilleas—
planted by the same pale hands
that shoved the iron links
down their grandfathers' throats.

Dice

As our stories settle, we travel
past fields and city streets, dusk
falling over the shoulders
of the passing day; memories
altered as counties disappear in
the rear view. I take the wheel
and imagine youth, pain-free—
skies of blue, luck of the good variety
in high abundance. That's you
in the corner, a smile as wide
as a canyon gulf; my eyes wrapped
around your every move.
We stretch and claw through our
daily routines; curse our fortunes
and toss dice at every wall
we come up against. Imagine us now,
in these towns and cities—life breathing
down our necks, laughing at the roles
we have chosen through the years.
Imagine the distance we shared—
light summer rain on our tongues—
time and space united; together
in one place the whole time

The Birthday Orange

SAMUEL CRADLED the orange in his hands and trembled. He did not dare to dip his chin and lower his eyes for a glimpse of the startling flash of color peeking through the gaps between his thumbs. He puckered his lips, containing his smile and swallowing the flutter in his throat. Samuel did not need to look. He knew it was there. He knew what it meant.

It meant that in Andalusia, Alabama, the fifth town in three years, the second in fourth grade, something had been different. He had still been the new kid in school, starting halfway through the year. He had still shuffled through the halls with his head down, neck hunched deep into the stretched rim of his T-shirt. He had still been the odd boy out in kickball, still partner-less for science labs, still eating lunch alone. Always alone. With his tomato sandwich and a table to himself.

And then he had meet Lucy. Long hair, straight bangs, whole galaxies of freckles. She went to a different school, the one across town where they wore knee socks and skinny ties, and she kept pet turtles and read books about Amelia Earhart and wanted to be a veterinarian when she grew up, or maybe an astronaut, and she kept her baby teeth in a little cardboard jewelry box in her dresser drawer and was secretly terrified of water, didn't know how to swim, and one day, down at Lake Jackson, Samuel had seen her standing at the weedy edge, fists clenched, the sandy water up to her ankles and he had boldly offered to teach her how to swim.

For five weeks during the glowing onset of summer, Samuel had waded into the tepid water with her, inch by inch, out of range of the tire swing cannon balls and squeals of *marco* and *polo*. By the end of June, Lucy could dunk him underwater and squirt mouthfuls like a fountain and float on her back with her dark hair in a scrolling halo around her face and call out the shapes in the clouds to him. One day they watched an entire fleet of puffy pirate ships sail lazily across the sky.

She was going to have a birthday party in July and asked him to come. He had paused mid-toweling, his hair still dripping into his eyes, and echoed her words. A birthday party. Yeah, dummy. With helium balloons and red velvet cake and a shoe-kicking contest on her swing set out back. He had nodded, awestruck, and stood for a while with his towel draped over his shoulders as he watched her flip up her kickstand and ride away.

Samuel had never been invited to a birthday party before.

He had run home to tell his mother and to ask to borrow five dollars for a present and then to ask what kind of present he should buy. His mother had turned to him from the kitchen table, opened mail stacked high against her wrist, an unfolded piece of paper in her hand and given him the look. She had asked him the date and then shaken her head. No. That's the day. We'll have to be out of here before dark.

But he had gone anyway. Breaking away as his family furtively stuffed boxes of dishes and trash bags of clothes into the back of the station wagon. He had gone tearing around the side of the house, then two streets over, across a scorched yard and over a wobbly chain link fence, until he arrived panting and heaving at the front door decorated with streamers. Lucy's mother had eyed him suspiciously, but opened the door to him and beyond her, in a kaleidoscopic room shimmering with shrieks, he saw Lucy amidst a circle of people, a paper crown on her head, and her eyes lit up when they alighted on him and she smiled and waved.

He had stood in the doorway, bent over, his hands gripping his thighs, catching his breath, and then he heard the station wagon's horn blaring unmercifully behind him. His parents had found him and he knew it was time to go. Lucy had run skittering across the tile, grinning widely, but when she had seen his face and the boxes piled high in the car behind him, she knew it too. They didn't hug. They didn't say goodbye. She had picked an orange from a bowl in the hallway and handed it to him. Thanked him for coming to her party.

Now, in the back seat, on his way to somewhere else, Samuel clutched the orange and he knew it what it meant. It was proof. Once he had been invited to a birthday party. Once, he had made a friend. And no one could take that away from him.

If I Were a Potter

I'd shape a bowl
bigger than a punch bowl but not so large
I couldn't carry it safely in my own two wrinkled arms.

I'd glaze my creation September Morning Blue.
When I see sky that color, I feel the day's embrace.
If I could make a bowl, I'd place it on this

cracked oak table, in sunlight. I'd pour
my sorrow there. My deep blue bowl
would hold the entire dark spill.

No longer would my sorrow cling to my every move.
When it leveled out and began to sparkle,
I would return to my wheel.

Back to School Night

Dear Scout,

I hope you don't mind me calling you Scout in front of your teacher; whoever that is going to be. I think this note is still beyond your reading level and someone will probably be reading it to you. All the parents here are doing this and it is a cute idea even if I suspect this is being done to kill some of the time here tonight because you don't have a teacher yet. I bet you are surprised to be hearing this letter. Your mother was surprised too. To see me here, that is. I've stayed across the room from her the whole time and haven't even tried to approach her. She did a great job of not blowing up at my being here. I'm glad there are plenty of other people around, all neutral parties as far as I can tell.

With this sheet of paper being pretty small, I see that I am going to need to write smaller to fit everything in. This may make it harder for the person reading this to you, but I think they're low on paper supplies. OK, here it goes:

Welcome to first grade! I hope this all turns out all right for you. I know this isn't the Citrus Valley Country Day School and that none of your friends are here. With your having two homes now we had to make some changes. We needed to save money. It was only after we enrolled you at the last minute that we found out your new school is using a wing of a storage unit facility as their temporary location. They've assured us that you will still get plenty of sunshine and will be able to play outside. They have plans to jackhammer out a space in a corner of the parking lot and put in a little grass area and maybe a tree. Your class will have a full-time teacher next week, as soon as the person's drug test comes back clean.

Coming in tonight a lot of the parents looked skeptical about this setting. I think your mother was, but like I said, I haven't even tried to approach her so I don't know for sure. They seem to really want to make a go of it here. I didn't know a storage unit could look as good as this. Some art, a couple of maps and some splashes of color have gone a long way. They need to work on the smell though. I keep smelling faint traces of rotten cantaloupe and what I think might be turpentine. Most of the people just quietly nodded when the principal gave his State of the Union-type introduction. One parent looks like a real jerk though, sitting there in his tasseled shoes, salmon tie, and big watch, tapping away at his phone while we're trying to listen. That, and his son goes by Bobo. Are you friends with that kid? I hope not. I know all your classmates are only six years old, or maybe seven, I'm not sure. Regardless, that is already too old to go by Bobo.

I hope you will still be able to follow this letter now that I am writing along the outside edges and I may have to do that on the back too. Just keep following the arrows. That guy though, jerk that he may be, is a dad. I see that there are uncles and cousins here subbing for dads who are in prison or God knows where else. Don't worry son, that isn't going to happen to me. I hope your mother told you that. Right now she's looking at me like all of this is entirely my fault and she may be right. She is glaring at me, making me fully realize that this is a horrible mess you are in and we have put you in a horrible place to get an education and spend your days. This isn't what we planned and this isn't at all what we aspire and hope for you. You have to believe that. We will fight for you. We will get you into a better school, but it won't be CVCDS. I am afraid that that just won't work again. You were so happy there. I am so sorry. Please forgive us and please believe me that we will try to make this better.

Love,
Dad

AMY RIDDELL

Mother's Requiem

After Natalie Diaz's "When My Brother Was an Aztec"

When my father was a stalker, he carried a gun
    and shot my mother every night.
        Sometimes he shot her in the eye

so she could see only half what he was doing to her.
    Mostly, he aimed for her heart so she would love no one
        but him. Each assault was ruthless,

but by breakfast, she would live again, wondering
    how much more she could take. If my mother tried
        to run, she would get a bullet in the back.

If she tried to stay, she would take one in the face.
    She didn't know which way to turn.
        Before he was a stalker,

my father was a mythical war bird thundering off the deck
    of a massive ship in the South China Sea.
        His voice boomed

in the heavens over Vietnam where he dropped
    cluster bombs and napalm on my mother
        even though she lived a world

away in Florida with us children, my two sisters and me,
    who didn't know she had been shelled to rubble,
        her roads and bridges impassable,

her fields fallow, her livestock left to rot. She didn't think to hide
    like the ravaged villagers who burrowed underground.
        She was younger then, stronger,

and we could have helped her, but she thought my father
    was only a man, not a god who could collect stars
        in a cup and drink their magic,

and rain down fire and pronouncements,
    and claim dominion over everything he had ever
        touched or seen or wanted or imagined.

She could not know he would return home a fallen angel,
    not disgraced, but clipped, his power
        only a faint aftertaste on his tongue,

his cluster bombs and missiles and napalm replaced
    with a payload so piddling it could fit
        in a single fist and a weapon so bereft

of fortitude that he could hold it steady with only one hand.
    She could not know he would look to her for his lost
        potency and stalk her as if she kept it hidden

from him in the hollow under her tongue
    which spoke his name softly, again and again,
        even as he reloaded his gun.

Adho Mukha Svanasana and Murder in the Retirement Community

My next-door neighbor got murdered.

My mom found out during yoga.

The guy who got killed was a sixty-year-old biker who used to have trouble doing downward dog, so he'd do child's pose while all the old ladies stood there with arms shaking like earthquake donkeys.

His son stabbed him forty-two times with three different kitchen knives. The strange thing, for me, is his switching utensils mid-murder, as if with each stroke he was judging whether or not he could accomplish something more efficient.

I went to the yoga class once, when the murdered guy was there. His son was there too, the murderer.

I remember them both in the back of the class, the feel like they didn't believe in any of this stretching crap, but that they had nothing else to do, that they were killing time until the drama would happen, that for now they'd just enjoy the air conditioning and holding back their hatred for all these old people who believe in everything so damn easily.

Why Do Houses Creak?

My wife has a gun in the bedroom.

It's in her hand now.

She won't let me touch it.

There's a noise downstairs.

The house creaks. The metal contracts more than the wood. It's been a fairly warm day. The unfortunate night has overdosed on freezing cold.

That's my guess.

She walks in front of a wall that looks like it has trichinosis. Or, no, she said it looks like it was "painted the color of trichinosis." I'm not sure what color that is, the wall having different shades of pus-yellow and death-white depending on the light, the sun, the season.

The gun isn't loaded.

Or maybe it is.

She tells me it's always empty. Because the statistics show that a gun is used for domestic homicide or suicide twenty-two times more than it's used for the mythology of self-defense, the great narrative that you get to defend your home, fearlessly, from some combination of rapist-rapper-terrorist.

She steps into the poison of the hall, so much weight on her thin shoulders, her life now in this moment filled with misogyny and class warfare and demography.

She disappears into the shadows and I'm left with the force of sound, the grief of waiting with only fists and thoughts.

MARISSA ROSE

Displacement

I didn't know what you meant
until after the funeral was over,
your mother and sister at the dining table
lighting cigarettes, one after another,
smoke surrounding their heads
like a mourning veil.
Your sister, whispering
that she couldn't do it yet, couldn't
push past the doorknob into your room
and pull to pieces the world
you'd left behind: socks heaping
over the hamper, half-full sodas
on the nightstand, orphan key chains.
I knew then what an intruder I was.
Still, sitting there, imagining
an untouched vacuum of things
so heavy no one could pick them up,
I felt everything I knew I had missed
in knowing you. Forgive me, then,
for the guilt I've carried around
in the years since I sat beside
the ones who loved you best,
wishing for a key or a hair clip of yours
to wrap my fingers around,
for a pocket to keep it in.
I only wish I'd known
the weight of you displacing
the lightness of my hand, the shape
indented in my skin as if it always was,
like you'd been my own.

What He Wrote

On the Sunday school chalkboard: P A N T I E S.
We were seven or eight, mine were thick
pink cotton with laced edges.
PANTIES. His name was Seth
and his face was always red and spit
dribbled from his downturned mouth.
Maybe he knew one day his redheaded
sister would drown, age 6, in the pool
at Camp Amity, no one noticing
until it was too late, her voice no longer
to dance the sanctuary of Bethesda Baptist.
PANTIES. Pants in the diminutive,
made girly for the sake of separation.
Bethany will never sing on earth again
and I'll never say panties again,
and I bet Seth's had a heart attack by now
or stands behinds bars, the clack of the slamming
doors making him grin at the man in the bunk
above. PANTIES still written in white chalk
in that Sunday school room in rural Georgia,
while nearby a haphazard stack of unused hymnals
grows dusty.

Underfoot

Shiny vinyl peel-and-stick
twelve inch squares, faux slate
in shades of brown and rust,
lay randomly inserted among

original linoleum—matte
and scuffed tiles of beige
flecked with white.
The tread-worn floor

remembers generations
of Masons meeting, their secrets
preserved. The new tiles
know nothing yet.

TERRY SAVOIE

A Mizzling Midmorning in the Bookstore Café

No end in sight
   to this rain, now

day & night all week long.

   It must come from
some very great distance.

   The elderly gentleman

seated at a next table,
   who's been doggedly

translating Boethius

   this past hour,
turns to me & whispers,

   "This, I suppose,

is just the sort of painful rain-
   fall we're likely never

to forget," & then

   dutifully returns to
what he hopes might be

   his philosophical consolation.

JAN ZLOTNIK SCHMIDT

A Gift: Kentucky Nursing Home—Many Years Ago

IT WAS A QUIET late afternoon in early winter, close to Christmas. She was there to hear their stories, give them back their pasts. The fluorescent lights in the room were dim, and the shadows of their bodies were etched on the lavatory green walls. They circled her waiting, walkers aside, bodies hunched, gnarled fingers gripping their knees. There was a hush in the room.

Then their stories:

"I ate burgoo, squirrel, possum. My daddy shot woodchuck, duck and made the stew."

Another—"The sap from the maple was yellow, honey gold."

And then muttered words: "There were coconuts in the trees we picked." A vision of thick palm leaves amidst redbud and magnolia.

She took a breath. Nodded. Although used to dementia, she was startled. Resisted the urge to say "really."

Then an old man in denim overalls, straps loose on his shoulder bones, shuffled toward her, scratching his bearded chin.

"Here for you."

He opened his palm. In it a greasy barbecued pork chop.

"Here a gift."

She choked down laughter, looked down. Ashamed of her response.

"Oh thank you. Thanks so much."

"A Christmas gift for you."

He stretched out his hand, and she put the chop in her flannel-lined pocket, grease staining her black pants and thigh. She held onto it for the rest of the session. Afraid to break the spell. Not wanting to leave his world. The world she was a stranger in. After all, Christmas was a time for miracles.

Or she was young then.

Giornata

we drink on bar stools, lounge beneath crepuscular
lights, locate the familiar placements of our cardboard
coasters, sketch each other's likenesses in blind

contour, he says: I know you didn't know
her, but here's to my Aunt Ramona

we clink beers and meditate on her suicide

I bow my head, inspect his sucking chest wound
how an archaeology professor might caress the glossy
orbits of a bleached white skull, seeking an identification

as I continue to listen, I picture an artist dodging
her ceiling fresco's terminal drip of wet lime plaster,
all of her half-painted antediluvian, cerulean cloud-sitting
figures scoffing back, their colorless fingers touching

like so many questions to answer, she was dying
from breast cancer, killed by a headshot wound, he asks:

you know how there's a core group of people
who you can actually talk to within your extended family?

...well, he says: she was one of those people

I worry about his heart, his myocarditis
his pregnant cousin, his taste in comic books
but sometimes all we need to do is laugh

smoke the cigarettes we shouldn't smoke
walk slow, round the corner sidewalk
wait in line for General Tso's and spareribs

California

It was easier
to love you
from a distance,

harder with the heat
of your breath
rolling off
my neck.

In spring
I left you wet
and growing

but summer
stripped you:
foothills bare
and sloping

like the muscles
of a man
stooped over
the sink

washing me out
of his mouth.

DAHLIA SEROUSSI

Everyday Darkness

A year under the clouds
turned my hair darker brown,
my skin, fairer than ever before.

A lifetime of year-long California
summers, so quickly lost
to this northern state.

I am becoming someone
I no longer recognize.

A wedding invitation arrives,
decadent cursive on the envelope—
I leave it unopened for days.

News of another friend expecting.
Alone at the kitchen table
I am crying—first happy

then enraged by my empty
coffee pot, refrigerator, cupboards,
my empty unmade bed.

Forsaking Forsaking

It's just workplace chit-chat. Just two married people,
not to each other, sharing emailed innuendos, winkies

and hallway high fives that slide slowly along their palms.
It's just enjoying a few laughs at lunch or when the sun shines

that especially warm yellow as the river cools the meandering
of their shaded conversations. It's just a couple of good friends,

whose fingers lace easily as they walk, taking longer each day
to hug each other goodbye. It's just two close friends texting

at midnight, making sure everything is still OK. It's just the way
they fill each other's newly discovered empty spaces. It's just two

people, married to strangers really, who now know everything—
even that neither can dream these days without closing their eyes.

DAVID SLOAN

That Chicken Bone

in our teenage throats? We tried
to breathe in stars on summer nights
at the lake, sat dangle-legged on the dock,
blue gills lipping our toes, conjured girls
tasting of tangerine and recklessness.
Later we longed for fingers small enough

to turn snapdragons into puppets,
for whistle grass, one more hot cocoa
with the blind lady down the block,
whose sly finger was the secret to never
overfilling a mug. Now it's the feeling
of always being left behind,

of people disappearing every day.
Some go grain by grain, some just seem
to vaporize, mist wraiths on a lake.
Others, like the blind lady, slink away
in the middle of the night. I don't know
which is worse, a sudden trap-door

poof that leaves an agitation of rain
and an amputee's itch, or the gnawing away,
a rat behind the ribs. Either way, you're gone,
except for the yearning and an audible absence.
It haunts every breaking day, a breathless
strain: *Death is for the living*.

DAVID SLOAN

Giving Voice

In the starless dark, we lie
splayed like starfish or halved

apples, four decades on,
your left leg thrown over my right,

as if in casual intimacy,
but nothing these nights

is thoughtlessly done.
In the starless dark, I'm groggy;

You're voltaically awake,
bursting with the blessing

of still being a daughter,
worried about our own,

trussed to a man who struggles
turning ideas into trees,

worried about all the children
who seem to be plummeting

down wells they've dug and lined
with stones from their own gardens.

In the starless dark,
your Courvoisier voice

still soothes, even as you churn
galaxies into fretting vortices.

Of all our attritions,
it seems the most imperishable,

deep reaching to deep,
sounding the way when it's time

to stumble companionless
into the starless dark.

Film Noir

He knows they will come, reasons death awaits us all,
listens asleep fully dressed lit by pulsing neon,
tuned into anything different from the usual
approach of crazy skidrow bums' distinctive tread,
howling flophouse dreams, sad hope turned to ashes
in rooms with bottle, grimy glass, bare light bulb décor,
narrow beds, pillows rancid with despair or dread.
A dog barks. He remembers her body under her mink,

stubs a *Lucky,* wishes he had a piece, stupid, stupid,
his cut from the shakedown going, almost gone,
grand plans drained like blood from a bullet hole.
At the window he hears the dog again, a cry in the night.
A sloped sill reaches a drainpipe, grouted bricks
afford knotty fingertip holds if he doesn't look down.
Down is the problem, inching down, his direction
until he can run, hide, slide no longer.

IAN C. SMITH

Selective Communication

If you call you'll get my machine.
If I'm not in the bath soaking aches,
matching wits with a wily crossword compiler,
or on the loo revising wasted days,
the lightning speed of the past,
or outside rejoicing at distant snow on summits,
walking a light-bathed terrain of eucalyptus scent,
memory trail of children grown, dogs long dead,
I might pick up,
but don't bother calling if you don't care for me.
You could interrupt me imagining another lifetime,
a romantic, almost unbearable waste of hours.
I remain busy in my own fashion,
try to avoid wretchedness where love went awry,
heartache from self-inflicted wounds, unhealed,
freezing me always on the brink of nothing much.
I keep to myself but not because I'm rude.
I also keep secrets, particularly my own,
content to read words polished to a shine,
also at ease, to a degree, with my own mind,
not believing I'm mad, but uncertain,
bound by idiosyncratic rituals making little sense.
If no light glows please don't disturb hard-won sleep,
dreams' surprising scenarios.
Whatever you want it can probably wait.
If I wake I'll consider the new day a bonus.
I should have died a thousand times.
I'll fumble switches; kettle, computer, rusted brain.
OK, I'll think, bring on what's left.

Say Its Name and It Will Come

He stands at the top of the maypole
and watches the children spin round
in circles, ribbons weaving together
like an ancestry of ghosts, a lineage
born of bright colors and dancing.

The village calls it the darkest May
Day in history, speaks of a haunting
just past the tree line on the far side
of town, grass bending and flattening
underneath a shrill wind song.

His walking stick becomes a scythe,
wax coat and oil cloth a black robe.
The words *plague doctor* condense
and rewrite themselves *reaper*.

He is not a human being
in their stories. No one had ever
even seen the face of the man.

They remember only hollows dark
as pitch where his eyes should be,
beak sharp and curved as a sickle,
the scent of garlic and camphor
wherever he walked.

If he ever had a name, it is gone.
Was he even a man? Who could say?
Now they call it *Pesta. Memitim.*
Azrael. Santa Muerte. Death.

The story crosses oceans and fords
rivers, learns how to tell itself

in every language. At the center
a birch tree and children and song.

A village on its knees.

His Grandkids Had Never Seen Him Like This.
He Had Never Worn a Beard.

Walt had asphalt for skin
despite the wide-brimmed hat
most assumed he had
never taken off.

His eyes narrowed from
the sweat and the sun
until he forgot what it was
to see a thing without focus
and furrowed brow.

The morning after he sold his house
on the hill, the one he built with
his first and last love, he woke
to buttercups and irises on his chin.

When he walked outside, bees buzzed
around him, a thrumming cloud.
Hummingbirds stopped for a drink.

He held out his hand
and expected to see a branch
but it was only a nest
of arthritic knuckles.

A black-bordered lemon moth
landed and looked him
right in the eye. He remembered
a yellow dress and a picnic
years ago.

Spoke to the moth like it was
an old friend. Said goodbye
to the hill, the strawberries,
the green beans and the house.

Crossed the cattle-guard. Opened
and shut the gate one last time.
Walked out into the field with a basket
some bread, a pitcher of blackberry juice.

Sat on the quilt for a long time
before removing his hat
running a hand through his hair
and giving himself to the afternoon.

ANDERS M. SVENNING

Eight Minutes to Thanu

Chaos is sharp, but so is Mortimer Goldberg on the last day of his life. Mortimer dreams of the birth of his first son and Garbanzo beans and the circles of Hell. All the states of matter together at once, he realizes, is consciousness.

To relinquish: *verb,* to renounce or surrender
    re·lin·quish
    rə'liNGkwiSH/
    to relinquish the throne

Mortimer Goldberg has ricocheted up and over the hood of an oncoming Chevrolet. Gliding past cars, sirens screaming, Mortimer Goldberg and his mother are growing closer.

Pigeons and bells are circling above his crown. Mortimer's brain bleeding. All facets expunged, except mortality.

Thanu.

Zipping past trees and clouds and asteroids and comets are Mortimer Goldberg's ideas. All essential energies are being pulled from the body and into the crown. In the hearts of the two—Mortimer Goldberg and his mother—a likened resolution has been found. The exchange has taken place in the heart of the City; and his two eyes are closed, the third open.

An Act of Love

for Lisa Rappoport

The broadsides arrived today,
just moments ago. They look

delightful. Simple but elegant.
That blood red on that rich light

tan of the Fabriano Tiziano.
The lovely embellished ribbon

resplendent beneath the poem's
title. Your clear-eyed vision

engendering the precision of
the images in the poem just by

the sensual physicality of each
word handset along the length

and the width of the page.
What lusciousness for the eye.

As a master chef plates haute
cuisine, you forever stylize

the depth of the printed word,
pressed firmly on the surface

of each leaf of paper, not so
removed from an act of love,

or that of forging the truth, as
in the intaglio of that blind—

stamped rose, which is etched
without ink, but that, as if

by the magic of your hand,
intimates such a deep rich color.

MARK TAKSA

Empty Noon

This country tilts to metal muscles and wire voices.
Among men who gather at café tables,
as if work is gossip and tea, one man rests
his hand on the thigh of the other
and asks to borrow a portrait

he will display for a lady who might love an art lover,
or he offers to lend his key to a hidden villa
where his friend, an art thief, can auction his loot,

or he is a banker revealing his vault lacks cash
but bursts with promises of regime gold.
They touch, their faces too tight for full flesh.

A microphone scratches, weights
the empty noon with the longing of a man
whose wife has drifted to a drink in a desert.
Women with groceries hurry through the plaza,
too quickly to leave the linger of perfume.

Slight Returns

I THINK WHEN we die we do it all again backwards. Not in a creepy 82-year-old baby way, but in regards to our choices. All those moments when you look back and imagine "what if," those moments when you lose yourself for several minutes as imagination spiderwebs out. As you come back, there's a sense of aging. It's as if you've lived double time briefly. Maybe instead of living it out again death is an extension of this daydream, pushed to its most radical intensity, drawing out a handful of strands before tying off the thread, only to reach back and pick up the next dangling uncertainty. These small thoughts I keep unspoken. To talk would be to taint. Against conversation the dreams would dry up and burn off, water left to boil and forgotten.

These small thoughts I do not speak.

I ask from beyond the closed door, "Do you want coffee?"

I hear "Reading my mind" or "Really not the time."

I do not ask twice. I empty the grinds from yesterday, peel a filter, reach for the Maxwell House, and wait for the percolation to sound, to displace the silence, for the aroma to steam out the wrinkles of last night.

She opens the door. All her essentials are on and her hair is tied back in a tight ponytail. There is an air of efficiency about her this morning. If time is a flat circle, then we are pencil and compass christening a new page. Until now she was carefree, her hair down, its natural wave never ironed out. Her words were casual, talk that knew silence as an ally save for in anger, when she revealed her keen ear, knowing precisely the sentence that would harm most.

"Coffee?"

"Oh...sure."

"Cream or?"

"Just as is."

"Right, I forgot we..."

"Same as you."

"That's right."

After handing her the mug I move to the window. The view of the harbor is wide and brilliant. The cold morning light clean and refracting off every surface with blinding enthusiasm. She comes up behind me. Her touch moves from upper arm to shoulder and down again. Her hands are warm from the coffee. Blood neglects them; these outposts at the fringe of her rely on outside stimuli. She inhales deeply as if she is going to speak, but rather than words, a sigh empties her lungs of their original inclination. Weariness fogs up the glass in front of me. Her arm drops and her steps retreat back into the kitchen.

"Listen I should go."

"Okay...I'll see you out."

Her coat is on. Laces spinning between fingers.

"Last night was..."

"Yeah it was."

She leans in and kisses me; the compass spins bottom to top. The pencil is dragged back over the same true line—that line repeated over and again until the graphite breaks skin. The initiation, then a small withdrawal, followed by a renewed exuberance, a deepening that, once it has been announced, quickly gets cut short. I can taste the coffee and almost make out the dark hours. They are hinted at but unresolved as her lips close and eyes reopen. A small grin. A quick turn of the wrist.

"I'll see you soon."

I wonder. I wonder.

These thoughts I do not speak.

A small grin. A quick turn of the wrist. My fingers entwined to the hand that remains still. I lock and pull. She turns, presses into me, eyes upturned, glassy with sleep unshaken.

"Maybe one more cup?"

There is a stillness I can hear fracture.

"I can't my day is just...but next time."

An old cord, worried between fingers, frays. Distances grow large, but will there be a recoil or only taught coarseness, fibers unraveling.

These thoughts I do not speak.

A quick turn of the wrist. A small grin. I let go of her hand and reach for my boots.

"I'll go out too. I've got some things to do today."

She smiles a small "seriously?" grin. A hint of teeth, a hint of doubt.

"Sure, sounds good."

It's cold outside. I forget my jacket. An offshoot of a river can snake across a con-tinent. A tangent can last a lifetime.

These small thoughts I do not speak.

Mercenaries

Holding a steady beam was my job those mornings.
   A good light doesn't have a hole in it.

He entered into a game of death
   like a heron or some sort of Zulu warrior.

Equipped in oversized accoutrements and covered in DEET
   the footing well placed in and amongst the landmines
     and craters left behind by some old heifer.

The focus narrowed to two button-sized eyes glowing under my cast.

His weapon raised and with a swiftness lowered again.
   A cacophony of thuds and pitter-patters as the choir disbanded.
   "I got his ass," he whispered from 40 feet away, "...but I bent it."

We collect back at the bank to add to the score and reset.
   Only fourteen more tours and I'll relieve him from duty.

Back home, the cleanup begins of the blood and muck.

Bathed in saline, powdered down, and peppered
   —fried to a crisp. We pray.

This reward and the crusty parts of Skillet are my favorite.
   I would do war with this man any day.

MICHAEL TUGENDHAT

The Feeling of Acceptance

I have become what I've always wanted to become.
Accepted like a fruit seed to the crabgrass. Tetchy

and told it can't grow any further once it reaches
a certain prominence, told it has hit its peak. Cinched

its robe, one drummer replaced with two drummers
then a whole band, an entire parade.

An elephant chained to my son's dog tags
accepted into a war he didn't and couldn't accept;

me at home on the telephone, washing dishes
listening to light jazz spring from a stereo,

sterile till the day I die.
Then I get the magazine.

Copy #75 of the Kenyon Review: the *apologetic issue*
where I wrote a story that my son never came back

and my wife left me. And my dog died.
Touching my penis is like hearing a symphony play

but then I know I can't have another son and see
the tax I paid on the bottle of bourbon: a dollar

thirty-six cents. My heart skips when the phone rings
it's the Kenyon Review; assuring me I would get my payment

in exchange for a copy of my son's death certificate.
Knowing I would at least get one more bottle

to wash away all those old dreams.

Meteor Shower

Stuttering out of black, the abundance hushed
our small talk—how they kept coming—
sparks tearing deep air, luminous
wounds closing over as quickly
as opened, gone.

Someone wondered aloud what the ancients
must have dreamed when visited by such
visions, and we spoke of omens,
imminent revelations, the end,
another beginning

as we wandered time-space in our heads,
sitting in lawn chairs, gazing, the high
desert floor arriving under our feet,
a rare clarity coming into our
voices in the dark.

I'm still trying to see them, trying to see us
there together, but you've made it hard
with your going. I'm trying to
speak as when our words
became eyes.

Shhhh

My mother is blowing gently in my ear
to make a soft place for me to sleep
inside my pain. If she stops a moment
too long I wake in its clench,

        Being, but an ear
in a dark motel room somewhere
in Arizona, traveling somewhere
I no longer believe in.

And what could I do for her
in her final pain, but kiss the bones
rising through her hands and face
and listen, as I listen now,
for something back of all that is
and isn't said—a gate between
breaths, a path in the air.

To Feed the Feral

Greenish gold eyes frame me: threat.
How long did it take to break
the trust of eight thousand years?
She carries mute history,
her coat a genetic mash-up
of gray and orange patches,
dab of white on striped tail.
Is she wrong to fear this hand
that belongs to the kind who murder
their own in schools and churches?
Yet need draws us near,
though our hungers may differ.
I step softly, bringing bowls
of slaughtered fish, slowly hold
out my fingers to be sniffed.
She basks in sun-warmed grass
in this small piece of yard,
and long before she allows me
to stroke her neck, shoulders, back,
skin begins to gentle fur
as fur gentles skin.

Insular Time

Fall again. The oystercatchers take
their mystery underwing, the puffins
turn into prayers oversea.

They leave us unfledged.

Without them the rocks shrink in
on themselves and so do we.

You waddle away the slow mornings.
Work is still bountiful before winter's
here. The sea, once a field, becomes

wall again, like the ones we can't cross.

We withdraw in our tinderbox thoughts
It takes a while to settle, the nights

especially, when you shiver against
the back of my dreams and I lie awake,
staring out into a vale of mist

willing it to become real once more.

On the Way Home

An hour into Oregon, the thought of dust
all but brushed off by airport numbness
and the chance of taking flight.

Nevada's sands still linger
in an unseen place, perhaps.

You'll find them when you undress
one winter evening, the moon glaring
coldly ahead.

Or they'll rise up, a pack of memories
on some bright Dutch river or when you
peddle a thousand silver lakes.

You'll think of them, the rough-patched soul
of the desert, the sagebrush that just can't
be undone and that strenuous line of
mountains crying battle-born

at sundown when the world yet again
gives in to land and you know
home is what you round up along the way.

Considering Pawpaw

SHE MAY HAVE her shotgun but I got the pistol. Pawpaw stowed it in his top dresser drawer behind socks and cuff links he never wore, not being the kind to doll up. I'd seen him attend family weddings in a short sleeve shirt, no tie. Forget how he dressed, the munitions he had were what snagged me, what got passed down from his dad, who I only knew from stories Pawpaw repeated. The German Luger felt so cool up against the inside of my hand. My grip fit.

Lots of times when he was gone for the chemo I went in and held it, spun it, aimed it, tested hiding it in my hoodie's front pocket. We lived next door, he invited us in to the two family ranch Meemaw's daddy built. All these old folks we hardly knew, they haunted what we were keepers of. It was like a compound, like a Midwestern Southfork. Hand-me-downs, antiques, heirlooms—call them what you like. Me and my brother didn't need to earn a dime. The railroad stock alone had us set.

Without work, what does life want?

I stole the luger and he never asked. But I'd begged over and over enough to hear the story of how we came by it, the great grandfather who never fought wars but in Over-the-Rhine alleys delivered beer and made deals. His friends rimmed the inside of the inside, clued him in to all kinds of valuable shit. No doubt Pawpaw suspected my sticky fingers. Why didn't he call me out? Knowing that story funny business I gnawed on like gum licorice, he should've laid me flat and frisked me, tore my room up. Granted, his legs were out from under him by then.

Crazy Ma sits on the porch with the shotgun across her lap, sipping vodka lemonade at nine in the morning, daring one goddamned blackbird to peck at her new-seeded lawn. That pistol's in my top dresser drawer back of my socks. Pawpaw's in the ground.

ELIZABETH KIRKPATRICK VRENIOS

A Ledger Balanced

We pass you from hand to hand,
brush the image of your smile caught
forever in these dog-eared snapshots.

How luminous you are here
in the odd flush of a mid-winter afternoon.
For a moment we breathe you

back into our lives as we read
your writing indelible
in black-and-white composition books

you've stashed under the bed
not certain, we could bear to open.
Cross-legged on the patchwork quilt

we turn each ink stained page,
the words you wrote,
burn like numinous comets

through our hearts
leaving us blistered and hollow.
We can only keep the memory

of what has faded into final air,
your gesture here, waving us away.
A remembered memory

the color of buttons and dark violet,
presses heavy as the woolen coat
we hold and send our fingers through,

just to feel the space of your body,
where it once was flesh and warmth.
As we name each moment yours,

a silent promise passes between us
to un-mention you:
a ledger balanced and put away,

a solace of hymns jailed in our throats.

Bathing My Mother

I ladder her slacks, panties down,
sit her on the stool, help first one
thigh, then the other over the tub's side

they are awkward as boards. Her body
shrunk to its minimum. Vertebrae
knuckle up her back.

I sponge her hairless legs, her feet
of long bent toes, arms as delicate
as the underfed. Only her belly is firm,

stretched across the growing mass,
clear over the map of veins
moving blood as it can—skin

so thin it could tear. I do not want
to wash her breasts, mere folds,
like empty pillow covers.

Between two ribs from spine to chest
I follow the old scar. She sighs, *That's nice.*
I hand her the lathered cloth to finish—

In this I am too close.

CONNEMARA WADSWORTH

My Mother Made a Doll House for My Niece

The furniture she bought—the Persian rug,
claw foot tub, chartreuse pears and scarlet
cherries in a bowl of glass, the little kitchen's
electric light, living room shelves with real
leather books. Oh! the canopy bed!

My own dollhouse was metal with floors
of painted-on wood, painted-on rugs,
drapes unrustled in painted stillness.
Beds of matchboxes, spools for chairs,
no flower vases, no TV to watch.

My sad dollhouse people—cheap, too hard
to love. And after all these years envy could
lift me in its turbulence. How is it I can still
want those wishes to have come true, to be
caught like a curtain rising in a breeze?

ROBERT WALICKI

Rain Leader

(on running storm pipe under a bridge near Akron, OH, 1997)

When the only heat is from the coffee
at 5:00 a.m., and less than 4 degrees outside,
you'll learn to wear enough layers,
or better yet, keep moving.

Some biker dude will laugh, blow frost,
Marlboro smoke in your face.
First day, it's "Hey rookie" and "Don't look down"
It's lift this 8-inch, cast-iron pipe.

First day, It's "Go down to my truck and get
my pipe stretcher," and then you'll realize
there's no such thing four stories down.
First day, men will want to break you,

like they've been broken, their riverbed faces,
grizzled beards twisted like dry rotted wire.
Last night's whiskey, sweating from dirty skin
You will nearly lose your finger, when the ice forms

on the pipe, straps loosening, metal slamming flesh.
If you can make it past this, there's a Miller Genuine Draft.
There's a welder sitting next to you, buys the first round,
lays his steel hands on your shoulder

like the father who couldn't bear it.
If you can make it past tomorrow,
you'll have to trust the pig iron,
this foot width of rust,
and walk this I-beam, 50 feet of crosscut steel
falling into nothing. There's a strap that holds
your waist, a broken man who leads you.
He'll walk like a free man across four inches of steel.
He'll never look back.

Cell Mates

OUTSIDE, RAIN FELL in torrents on the little village of Innesquade and on the Dolahan, the old pub where assorted locals were slaking their thirsts. At a table in back by the hearth, four men of middle age sat where they usually sat, playing their usual game of seven card stud.

"Whose round is it anyway?" Big Liam spoke with asperity through his fantastical mustaches, his eyes narrowed.

"It's yours, you heap of shite," said equally large but plain-shaven Conchob, tapping his knuckles on the table. "But before you get up, I call you." He wiped a portion of the wet table-top with his sleeve and spread his cards on it. "Aces over twos."

"Fook me," said Liam as Conchob raked in the pile of coins. Liam then stood, extended his arms and gave such a howl that all the patrons at the bar turned around and looked at him.

"A veritable banshee," said little, bald Seamus.

Said Patrick who sat opposite Seamus, "A banshee's a she, last I heard." His long ashplant leaned against the wall, the top of it touching a broken brick on the hearth in which a peat fire smokily and fitfully burned.

It was Conchob who yelled across the room, "You been to Denmark lately, Liam?"

"Kiss me arse," Liam said, sticking his posterior out and patting it. He then pulled from his back pocket a billfold and looked therein, astonishment on his face, raising eyebrows that grew like an untrimmed thicket from one side of his pate to the other.

Conchob nudged Patrick. "Look at that, will ya. I do think the fooker's broke."

Little Seamus tried to wipe the wet off the table with the back of his hand. "Bring us a dishrag, will you?" he yelled to Liam.

"And a log for the fire," Patrick said, hugging himself for shivering.

"And your fooking fairy godmother," Conchob shouted.

A cell phone rang from the card-players' table, the theme from "The Valkerie."

Said Conchob to Seamus. "That would be your wife. Sure, you're pussy-whipped."

Said Seamus with a wink, "It isn't me wife at all; it's my mistress." He put the cell to his ear and said: "How do I love thee? Let me count the ways."

"If you got a mistress, I'm the fooking President of the fooking Republic," Conchob said, snatching the phone away from Seamus. "Hello," he said. "Who is it I'm talking to?" He paused, a squall of shock coming across his face. "Fiona??"

Conchob put his meaty paw over the phone. He looked at Patrick. "It's *Liam's* ball and chain." He squinted at Seamus. "You little devil, you." Then, he went back to the phone. "I'm afraid your better half is in a bit of a fix. He appears to be short on funds. I'm wondering if you have any suggestions as to how to remedy the situation?"

As Liam made his way slowly back with four fresh pints, Conchob said into the phone. "Oh, I couldn't bring myself to do such a dastardly thing."

Liam set the precious Guinness on the table.

"Here," Conchob said, "You can talk to himself yourself." The fierce rain without was nothing compared to shrieking from the cell phone. "Your lovely wife, I believe," Conchob said to Liam with a wink and a shit-eating grin.

"Hello," Liam said into the phone.

Said Patrick, "This ought to be rich."

Added Seamus, "I don't think this is his night."

"I'll be home when I get there," Liam told the phone. Then, "No, I took out a fooking home equity loan."

"Not with your digs," Conchob said.

Liam held the phone at arm's length, the howling coming from it like a burst of feedback from a faulty speaker. His eyes narrowed as he contemplated the instrument. He patted the side pocket of his trousers and then he looked at his friends. "Whose cell is this?"

Seamus pointed his finger across the table. "Sure, it's Conchob's."

"You lying little prick," said Conchob.

"So that's how it is!" Liam glowered at Conchob. "Think you can cuckold me?"

"I don't even own a cell phone," Conchob said.

Liam stood up suddenly, the cell phone falling on the table. "Get up, you big oaf. I'm going to knock off your head and send it clear to County Mayo."

Up then did Conchob get. "Well, if you won't listen to reason, there's a better way to settle this, once and for all."

And so, like their legendary forefathers Conn of the Hundred Battles and Cumhall, father of Finn McCool, at it they went with such furor that the very bricks in the hearth trembled and Patrick's ashplant fell clattering on the floor.

"And I'm after a strategic withdrawal," said Seamus, pocketing his cell and prancing his way like a little elf past the combatants.

And if anyone with ears sensitive enough to hear Seamus's voice under the din were to make a true report, he would have repeated what the little man said into his cell phone: "I love thee to the depth and breadth and height my soul can reach."

And then, pilfering an umbrella from the stand by the door, Seamus went out into the wet.

LISA WEISS

Sexy Wil and Shao-Ling

MY FATHER'S ON the phone. "They put shawling into the ground." That's what it sounds like, his voice closed, soft and low. I hear him say "burial," another intense word I don't know but like for the way it purrs, for the rhythm, for making me see red berries in my mind. Not interested, I'm only four, I turn away from his closed office door, but have changed it to "shawling out" because "o" sounds better with the word "shawl" than "i," more connected, and I whisper it to myself, "shawling out of the ground, shawling out of the ground," in love with the sound and feel of it. Back to whatever I was doing— playing with my things, lazing around the house, mother down in her kitchen.

I just care about the sound of it and the feel of it. Who cares what it means?

Delicatessen. Delicatessen. Delicatessen. I say these words over and over at four, whispering them so nobody hears, the pleasure of them all mine, in my mouth and ears while I play.

Delica-tess'en: it makes me feel like I have to get someplace, like someone or something's pushing at me from behind, telling me I'm somehow supposed to be somewhere other than here. Five syllables, accent on the fourth, a quick breath after the fifth, and then hurry and return to the first, and repeat it, again and again. Never say these words out loud. They'll think I'm crazy. Breathily, I whisper it, anxiously, to myself, delicatessen, delicatessen, anywhere: in the family car, at the drive-in with mom and dad watching "Gigi" fall in love with a much older man, but in their case, surprise, they're really and truly in love.

Delicatessen. Shawling into the ground. They add up, mix in, as I grow up.

There was "Shantilly," too, another favorite.

Sh, Shh, Shush, Shantilly, Shawling, Delicatessen. (Keep it quiet.)

Eight years later, a letter, "Darling Shao-Ling," on my father's desk. I've stopped to scratch my ankle or something, and am standing over it, looking down on it. None of my business, and I'm not yet the least bit interested, at thirteen. Half folded, half out of an envelope. Mother's across the hall for a moment, gone to the bathroom. Shredding papers all afternoon. Sh, Sh, Shred, Shredding, Delicatessen, Shawling, Shao Ling. (Dad's just died.)

Sixteen years later, I'm twenty-eight. The bed creaks. Sexy Wil is what I hear whenever it creaks, while he's on top of me. Where was mom that winter night I bring Wil, eighteen, my piano student, to my old house, just for the oddball feel of it. We cook soup in the kitchen after making snow angels outside, then get into my childhood bed and make love. On my old dresser, the pink lace box of Chantilly toilet water still there, bottle still inside, contents evaporated.

Any time I'm back there now, visiting old mom, I lie there and the bed creaks if I move even a little, and I say Sexy Wil, Sexy Wil to myself, and Shhh, Shhhh, Gigi, lucky girl, truly in love, I'm just like Dad, creaky bed, sexy Wil, S-W, shaw/wil, sha-w-ling. Shao-Ling, delicatessen. Where am I going? Just like dad, I don't know. What'd mom know? I don't know. Who cares what it means? Wish I knew. I understand it all as some kind of symphony, and that's all I understand.

JILL WHITE

Grief Is a Foreign Country

Grief is a foreign country.
They do things differently here:
no immigration restrictions;
no return date on your visa.
Well-meaning tourists
pass through quickly,
pausing only to ask
how are you doing?

Residents live an overcast life.
Many shiver
in thin coats of memory;
others lie breathless, prone
beneath the weight of tomorrow.
Although the dawn prevails,
even the time zone is confounded
by hours passing
at the speed of evolution.

Agatha

*"Cruel man, have you forgotten your mother and the breast
that nourished you, that you dare to mutilate me this way?"*

Saint of bread and bells—nurses
and cancer, she bears her martyrdom
like strawberry sundaes on a plate;
embers, pincers, shears, tongs, veil—
virgin martyr, forgive our confusion
at what you carry on that silver
platter; that we see you as saint
of cupcakes and muffins, golden bells,
brass, bronze, foundries, and, of course,
volcanic eruptions.

Discovering a Noble Truth in the Backyard

after Charles Wright

Charred end of August, oven-dry heat
    lifting out of Mexico. Too much sunlight, for too long.
A dove coos once in the live oak, then again,
       the last time till spring. Your drink-cooled hand

Finds mine, and I hadn't realized mine was lost.
    Something gets caught in the throat, inaudible,
Ineffable. Something, daddy might say, better left unsaid.

     To understand that everything must go, sooner
Or later—you and I, the dove, the oak,
   the whole goddamn shebang—it's not the later
      that bothers me, but the sooner.

Dylan Thomas at the Writing Shed

Above the boathouse hill was a shed.
Dylan would find poems like schooners in the bay.
Such a window, no matter how small,
could always see what he needed to see.

From here, he could see the Tâf estuary.
The Gower peninsula was further beyond
in the Bristol Channel,
the shallows narrowing in.

There were caves in the peninsula
where archeologists found
the Red Lady of Paviland,
a skeleton dyed with red ochre.

He could almost see the menhirs
on the Gower. Those standing stones
had been upright since the Bronze Age,
and now only eight remained.

One was a twenty-five ton capstone
supported with upright stones
like lines stacked to support a poem's meaning.
Anyone could interpret the constructor's intention.

Sometimes all you need is the right tools.
All you needed was all the pain in the world.
After staring, Dylan labored over his poems,
rubbing red ochre into their fragile bones.

Dylan Thomas Chair, Looking Out the Writing Shed

White banners of egrets; lapwings'
slow irregular wingbeats, like a person
having a change of heart;
herons mating for life;
oystercatchers wading on the shore edges,
poking in the sand with long orange beaks;
seals sun tanning on gray rocks,
merging with local color.

The oystercatchers knew this secret:
the world was a bipedal cockle.
If you pried it open
from its hinges
beyond its saltwater taste,
you might find sheen inside
like the inside of a pocket watch
with all the time in the world
to create.

MARTIN WILLITTS JR.

Letter to a Son

When you outgrew my stories, you did not care
if I sang you to sleep, or watched over
the dreams on your face.

You were alright, traveling the difficult path
of children towards adult. There was no map.
You wouldn't believe it if I told you there was.

Ten times a night I would pace and perch
at every breath. Now I miss those opportunities.
You turn the pages of your own sadness.

You were never a burden. I carry the weight
of your infancy on my arm like a tattoo.
When I held you, all the stories and songs began.

Now I forget the stories, songs lose their melodies.
At this distance, tell me, are you alright? Tell me
you need me, as hours jump dreams like terrified sheep.

MARTIN WILLITTS JR.

My Father Smoldered Like a Campfire

I want to forget that night. I want life
to be a smooth stream. One of quiet
and purpose. However, rivers find rocks
and cause a collapsing sound, a rush
gathering strength and speed to get elsewhere.

I do not want to remember my father
saying, "Never straighten a crooked road."
My father would say odd things like that.
We would stifle his words like a campfire,
but his words would go ashen and seethe.

Perhaps he was trying out his voice
to see if it still fit him like matches in a box.
We would blink at his outbursts.
We never understood them
and while we analyzed them
he had moved like a tentative deer
to another strange idea, nibbling on it.

He said, "Never let rain fall upwards."
And sure enough, that night it rained up.
It was as if he had commanded it.

He did not talk like that all of the time.
We were concerned if this was genetic.
You'd never know when a switch
would flip, until his eyes tilted.

Sometimes he would thrash around
like a black bear tossing in trash cans.

The night he died, he said,
"It is never like they said it would be;
it is not a grand ballroom."

MARTIN WILLITTS JR.

Apples, Soup, Wooden Bowls, and Silence

Death comes with its own appointments and disappointments.

A man was blowing across the spoon of hot soup.
He had lived his whole life in the same house
inherent in its silent mysteries.

There were apples on the ground only a goat could love.
Windows could open for sparrows to ghostly fly in.
If he took any book out and read it again,
would he press his tongue inside his cheek,
concentrating sunbeams through old curtains?

Between picking and selling apples, and
pouring soup into his own handmade wooden bowl,
did he stare at the same small acre he had owned,
knowing its harshness
was a goat bleating up storms of snowflakes?

He thought he knew every square inch:
every mole hill; every thistle; every ragweed;
every apple tree—by its personal name.
No matter how often he studied,
he would find some new wrinkle in the grass,
some extra water in the pond,
some frog extending its legs through yesterday.

Death might have missed him
because he was quieter than silence.
However, he knew Death
was nonchalantly strolling through apple trees
when the leaves turned white.

He set aside the wooden spoons,
laying one on top of the other

like they were making love
on a blanket of pale-yellow daisies.

He greeted Death, the wooden bowls
clattering to the floor, dust already settling,
filling the top bowl with disturbance.

MARTIN WILLITTS JR.

Final Leaf

In certain slowness
the last leaf takes its final breath

we do not recognize its fragileness
is too much like ours

we could lay our hand on it
just to feel it jolt out of its silent waiting

this nearness of death
this separation

this world between living and dying
the crossing-over and surrender

we resist this temptation
to let go

Speak No Evil

THE STRIP of bleached sand between rock and water stretched further than his eye could see, narrow as a child's spine. Wind-born waves bounced on the water's surface, their foamy peaks rising and falling in pale-necked marionette nods. Even the bleak night sky glowed white, lit by an oblong moon leaking a fog of celestial vitreous.

The ranger's cabin was three miles away, over the lip of the next canyon.

The man would see nothing, even if he were awake.

A rope of thorny scrub knotted itself around the lake's forty-mile shore. He wondered how deep beneath its basin their twisted roots must lie, how tightly they squeezed in years that failed to provide enough rain. Could those roots feel the churning pulse of the water above as they sought out the cracks in those giant sheets of slate? When they knocked at the rock-lined lake bottom and crept through those cracks to drink from its depths, were they content with the first cold sips? Or did it only make them long for more?

He knew what his answer would be.

A sudden gust floated a noise that sounded like a whimper. He spun. Trees were the obvious culprit, but there weren't any—no gracefully weeping willows or strong, stalwart pines. The thorny lakeside scrub stood only as high as a tricycle. The lake's entire perimeter lay unprotected. Any human present would have to crawl to escape detection. *Would they?* he thought. *Would I?*

An animal, then. But diurnal creatures were what prowled these rocks and hills and trails. Moonlight couldn't warm the rocks enough to lure the diamond-backed lizards, tails longer than their stumpy bodies. Dry snips of grass couldn't tempt a velvet-eyed deer, tottering fawn in tow. Without trees, there were no bushy-tailed squirrels, skittering across brittle branches. Not a single creature whose wandering breath could replicate the sound he heard.

Maybe a bird? He looked up. The sky lay wide and empty, the dark underside of a toy box flung open and dumped upside down. No whistling beaks or flapping wings, no caws or coos or hunter's shrieks. It was past the season for hatchlings. If a desolate mother had abandoned her nest, those offspring would be in the belly of another by now. Even if she hadn't, one squealing chick might still meet the same fate, spotted by a hawk with sickle-sharp talons.

At his feet, the water gurgled and splashed onto his shoes. This was no sea. No moon-drawn pull created breakers that could sigh the way a human does, the way the ocean does when its full fathoms recede over rocks and sand and seaweed and moss and canyons deeper than the human eye can see.

Not one of these things could have created that wind-borne whimper. Not one of them could know what he had done. He looked up to the ridge, its ruffled green edge silhouetted against the sky. The ranger slept. They all did.

There was only one other creature who might have made that sound.

And only one who might make it again.

He bent down and slid off his shoes, hooking each index finger over a heel. Then he plunged his feet into water cold enough to numb the skin. To shut off all feeling, all longing, all desire and ability to obey the electrical impulses coded by bits of fiber string and protein wire wound tightly into shapes that meant he would be short or tall, dark or fair, good or bad. With every step, he whispered something over which he had no choice—brown, blue, short, thin, long, narrow, flat, wide, arched, proud, sharp, round. He saved the final thing, her name, for last.

Scribbled Paths

Bees never sleep in, especially when a stick
is jabbed in their hive. I ran, startling
some cows awake that hurriedly dressed
in mismatched patches of brown and white hides.

I climbed in and rolled up my windows. In scribbled paths,
the bees bounced their Epcot eyes against what I imagined was
a kaleidoscopic visage of me. Turn. Tumble. Torture.
Me behind glass for a change.

Through my windshield I saw two bushy eyebrows of hawks
twisting like ashes still adrift after a black blaze of night. They
circled slowly in the blue-white swirl
of that sweet slice of sky.

Cars backed up. I was the object of more and more
anger, of horns blaring, tending to longer
and louder.

Sir Isaac Newton. Wearing your curly girlie wig.
First magistrate of physics and expert on the curve of things.
Of wings, and winds, and gravities. Of such an imperturbable
pre-modern patience to still stare at me from a pixelated copy...
of a photo...of a painting...of you stiff in your library of thick-paged books—
as seen through the eyes of a long-dead artist with eyes
reborn through a twisting triangle of arrows
turned upon themselves. Nothing I see
remains at rest.

SHANNON K. WINSTON

The Electrician's Daughter

Forget the garden gloves, I love wires:
the short synapses and frayed cables
that ignite sparks in the basement.

Once, I held a light bulb in my hand
and thought the world could fit there too.
Its smooth, white surface curved like

a nest but more fragile. Bulbs
lit and fueled white on white.
I could never tell where one surface started

and the other began. My fingers slipped
and unmade what I secretly wished
would turn indigo, then burst into fire.

Legend

BONNIE AND I robbed a filling station in Hobart County, Kansas and it went well. It looked like we would make off with a loaf of fresh Rainbo Bread and several slices of pretty good bologna, the proprietor's watch, and twenty-some dollars and change.

This was during a particularly loud and teeth-rattling dust storm, one of many that plagued that corner of Texas, Oklahoma and Kansas. The proprietor, a Willis Hagg, asked how we could call ourselves Robin Hoods if we just stole from people trying to get by and I said we didn't advertise ourselves as any such thing. We took money democratically and spent it. It caused Bonnie to think, however, and she amended my proclamation with this:

"Mr. Hagg, we will double your money and send it to you after we rob a bank. This is just walking around money. An investment. Remember us as Bonnie and Hubert. We'll need some gasoline. We'll take care of that, too."

"Bert for short. No one calls me Hubert," I added.

"Bonnie and Bert. Well," said Mr. Hagg.

"That just doesn't work," Bonnie said. "Don't repeat it."

"Well," said Hagg.

The screen doors of the filling station slammed and rattled outside the regular doors.

"Why doesn't it work?" I asked Bonnie.

"I don't know. It just hasn't got zing." She looked at me with a new sort of appraisal. "And you're shorter than I am," she said.

It began to lighten up outside, and the wind had died down some. That's when Clyde Barrow slipped inside brandishing a revolver.

"These young folks has already got me for forty-some dollars, my railroad watch and some sandwich fixings," Hagg said to Barrow.

"Forty?" I had to question that.

"After the bank job. To keep your Robin Hood legend good and solid," Hagg said.

Barrow had been quiet during the exchange, but the pistol in his hand was steady and searching for a target. Once he had us figured out he aimed it at me and said, "Gun please. I'm Clyde Barrow. Remember that name."

I turned it over without relish. I never liked being unarmed.

"And you are?" Barrow addressed this to Bonnie.

"Bonnie Parker. Of Bonnie and Clyde. Now that has zing, you see?" She said that last bit to me, but her eyes were locked on Barrow's.

It was an important moment, anyone could see that. And, outside, be damned if a dirty rainbow wasn't arching over the store and the road that Bonnie and Clyde took toward their short and lively time together.

Hagg coldcocked me and that's the last thing I remembered, that rainbow and them scooting off in a dust cloud, before waking up in the Hobart County jail. Hagg's place was the jail, post office and a sort of general store. He took possession of the 1928 Ford Model A Bonnie and I had driven up in. He said, "You are just not a legendary sort, Hubert."

"Bert. Call me Bert."

Pie

MY MAMA blows in, storm that she is, and says she wants her some blueberry pie. I say, "Girl, you haven't talked to me in ages. How you gonna come at me like that?" She says, "I'm still the mama in this drama and you, dear girl, ain't shit."

This kind of talk was so much of my childhood, you have no idea. She says if it weren't for her drunken whorin' ways, I never woulda even happened. I'm just what she got for liking sex and liking it where and whenever. Couldn't point to my daddy for a million, trillion bucks.

Further, she tells me she was all tart perfume and miniskirt and sashayin' her ass into the nearest bar and doin' it in the men's room. Right above the toilet which is where I was probably made.

Then she asks, "You gonna get me that pie or what?"

Bia

SHE SAYS, "as in my life story. As in *bio*. Only I'm female."

"Oh, I get it." Got the female part when she entered my office. Bare summer legs. Thighs sturdy as tree trunks.

"Where did it start," I ask her. "This *bia* of yours."

"Well," she says, "my parents met on the Internet."

"Not that far back," I say. The air smells like her perfume. Like apple. Like some-thing I want to bite.

"All right," she says, moving her tree trunks under her miniskirt. "Ten minutes ago, I bought this coffee. Now I'm here."

I like her. Want to hire her. But I futuresee where this is headed.

"Give me something in between. Like where you went to school. What qualifies you to work here?"

"Vassar," she says. "I take breaths on an ongoing basis. And I see no other applicants."

She is quite correct. Word must have spread about the difficult interview questions.

I take another look at her tree-trunk thighs. Take another whiff of apple.

I hire her then and there. "Let's get back to your *bia*," I say. "What website did your parents meet on?"

All the Babies

I could have been. Take, for example,
my mother's first boyfriend. Sweaty,
geometry hands. Well, someone had
to date him, she would later say. I
liked her for that, but I was happy
he wasn't my father. Or the next one,
Hank, a nice boy, but sick. Epilepsy,
my mother would whisper. Anyway,
he died six months later. Suicide,
though she couldn't say the word.
But, then, there was my father, handsome
stranger. *Roseland* on a restless August night.
They went out once and he didn't call
back. She told me she was ready
to let it go. But maybe I was
in the air around her head. Wordless
spirit hovering as she sat there, ignored.
Nudging her against her better judgement,
pushing her invisibly to pick up that phone.

Summer Story

Wet sand and seaweed gook. Tide creeping under your salt-bloated toes.
Last night's bonfire ashes smoking towards the sky.

The beach house behind you is a slapdash of woodbones. Every so often a window.
Open enough for airfingers to slip in and stroke you lover-like.

And speaking of lovers—where did yours go? Last night his full moon face
in the bonfire light, then later, hovering above you, behind you, under you.

Last night, he built a sandcastle. Then he showed you the sandcastle.
Then he was the sandcastle.

You'll understand if he ever comes back. Just watch as the seafingers stroke him
away at low tide.

Convenience

Suppose it's Thursday, and you're driving home
from picking up your husband, who decided
he didn't feel like bowling after all, like he usually
does. *No reason,* he says, and you know better

than to ask. You pull into the parking lot.
Milk for tomorrow's breakfast. Morning will
smack the sun back in the sky, and your husband
will be yours again for awhile. By the time
you're in the dairy aisle, you're certain he's texting

his girlfriend. Phase out stage, and you know this
by the way he's been nuzzling you in the middle
of the night. Just like the last time and the time
before that. And as soon as you dropped
your guard, he was done with you

again. Now, you pick up a carton of milk,
check the expiration. Good for another day.
Outside, the girl is probably texting back
What's wrong or *what did I do.* He will
tell her *nothing,* the way he'll be
telling you a month from now.

You want to hate this girl, find her name
in his unguarded cell and track her like a dog,
but the truth is, you're as bad as she is,
loving a no-good man, unable to walk away.
You feel more like a painsister
than a wounded wife, and when

you step back into the parking lot, see him
stashing his phone in his pocket, sliding
into the driver's seat, you know again
that a carton of milk is all
you can admit to needing.

Wednesday

Charley says it's too schizo
and would it please make up
its mind. *Is it coming from
last week or going towards next?*

I can see the division in Charley's
eyes. Two into seven is three
and a half. *The whole damned week
is coupled off,* he says. Thursday

and Friday, gift-wrapped and tinsel,
then Saturday, Sunday, wine-soaked
and cool. Monday and Tuesday,
drudgebucket days, but at least

they have each other. Sometimes,
I feel like Wednesday. Leftover,
halved, when Charley slams out
to find the part of himself he left

in the world. Alone, I just make
dinner, mid-week mash of cornflakes
and canned soup. Even my foods
don't go. But on some of those

nights, before Charley gets home,
I prop him up, invisible. I whisper
the question, *coming or going?*
Outside the window, a goldenrod
moon is steering real-life Charley

toward whatever it is he's looking
for, while back inside, here, couch
cushions sink with Charley's absent
weight. And me, holding my breath
as I wait for his answer.

Silence in F Sharp Sustained

The architect in the natural light of his setting:
He wants his buildings bathed in it, hoping
they'll stand the better for it. He builds boxes
out of darkness, each designed to cast a different
shadow: morning different from afternoon
different from fire and fluorescence, as different
from incandescence as sunlight reflected
off the moon. And there are different kinds
of darkness like degrees of gray in a Richard Hugo poem
depending on the box's position relative to
a stationary observer, the shape of the box
and the quantity of light let in through doors
and apertures. Music, on the other hand, punctuates
various kinds of silence with various kinds
of sound. And the repertoire of sound is
just as varied as the many kinds of silence:
Some correspond to the various thousand-fold
layers of contemplation. Others are created
by absence. The silence in the box when the world
outside rages. The sounds by which we measure time.
There are silences of houses at night with
people sleeping. Sounds of houses with
no one home. Sounds in houses like the silence
of death. Silence music makes us long for
just as we sometimes hunger for light and shun
the box the architect puts us in. And the sounds
of certain birds are the sounds of silence.
And the absence of sound is not the absence of noise.
Maybe the silence of the slaughterhouse
screams at the silence of conscience or at the
silence of science where silence itself screams.
The silence of plant life. Whole histories
written and read in the dark without sound.

CONTRIBUTORS

Stephanie Bryant Anderson is author of *Monozygotic|Codependent* (The Blue Hour Press 2015). Recent or forthcoming publications include *Tinderbox, burntdistrict, Vinyl,* and *The Blueshift Journal.* Besides poetry, she enjoys kickboxing and math. Stephanie is founder of Red Paint Hill Publishing.

Diana Anhalt, originally from Mexico, is the author of *A Gathering of Fugitives: American Political Expatriates in Mexico 1947-1965* (Archer Books), three chapbooks—among them *Second Skin* (FutureCycle) and *Lives of Straw* (Finishing Line), in addition to essays, short stories and book reviews in both English and Spanish. She placed first in the Georgia Poetry Society's contest for their annual collection, and her work was nominated for this year's Pushcart Prize. Her book, *Because There Is No Return* (Passager Press), released in August, is now in its second printing.

Anne Babson's first collection, *The White Trash Pantheon,* was published last year by Vox Press. Her work has appeared in journals on five continents. She has won multiple poetry prizes and has residency grants from Yaddo and Vermont Studio Center. Her blog, *The Carpet Bagger's Journal,* has over forty thousand hits. Her opera libretti are being performed in 2016 in Boston and in Montreal.

Pam Baggett's poems appear in *Atlanta Review, Crab Orchard Review, Kakalak, San Pedro River Review, Tar River Poetry, The Sow's Ear,* the anthology *Creatures of Habitat, Forgetting Home: Poems About Alzheimers,* and *The Southern Poetry Anthology Volume VII: North Carolina.* A Pushcart Prize nominee, she teaches writing workshops and co-hosts the Second Thursday Poetry Reading at Flyleaf Books in Chapel Hill, NC. Her garden book, *¡Tropicalismo!,* was published by Timber Press. She lives in the country outside Cedar Grove, NC.

Rebecca Baggett is the author of four chapbooks, and her work appears in numerous journals and anthologies. Recent work appears in *Atlanta Review, Miramar, New Letters,* and *Southern Poetry Review.* She lives in Athens, GA.

Bobby Steve Baker lives in Lexington, KY, with his wife, multiple male offspring, and a very large Airedale. He has published poetry in *Bop Dead City, The Ann Arbor Review, Kentucky Review, Cold Mountain Review, Linnet's Wings,* and many others. His latest book of poetry and art is *This Crazy Urge to Live* by Linnet's Wings Press.

Mary Jo Balistreri has two books of poetry published by Bellowing Ark Press, and a chapbook by Tiger's Eye Press. She is presently finishing her fourth book of poems. She is a founder of Grace River Poets, an outreach for schools, churches, and women's shelters.

Roy Bentley is the author of ten chapbooks and four books of poetry, including *Starlight Taxi* (Lynx House Press, 2013). Poems have appeared in *The Southern Review, Shenandoah, Prairie Schooner,* and, most recently, in the anthologies *New Poetry from the Midwest* and *Every River on Earth.* He has received fellowships from the NEA and the arts councils of Ohio and Florida.

Bryce Berkowitz is an MFA candidate at West Virginia University. His work has appeared or is forthcoming in *Passages North, Oyez Review, Oxford Magazine, Evansville Review,* among other publications.

Adam Berlin Adam Berlin is the author of the novels *Both Members of the Club* (Texas Review Press/winner of the Clay Reynolds Novella Prize), *The Number of Missing* (Spuyten Duyvil), *Belmondo Style* (St. Martin's Press/winner of the Publishing Triangle's Ferro-Grumley Award) and *Headlock* (Algonquin Books of Chapel Hill). His stories and poetry have appeared in numerous journals. He teaches writing at CUNY's John Jay College in New York City and co-edits the literary mag, *J Journal: New Writing on Justice.* For more, please visit adamberlin.com.

Nancy Bevilaqua's poems have appeared in or are forthcoming from *West Branch, Whiskey Island, Tupelo Quarterly, Hubbub, Hermeneutic Chaos, Tinderbox Poetry,* and other journals. In late 2014, she published a collection of poems entitled *Gospel of the Throwaway Daughter.* A native of New York City, she now lives in Florida.

A German-born UK national, **Rose Mary Boehm** lives and works in Lima, Peru. Author of *Tangents,* a poetry collection published in the UK in 2010/2011, her work has been widely published in US poetry journals (online and print); she is twice winner of the Goodreads monthly poetry competition; a new collection of her poetry is earmarked for publication in 2016 the US.

Ace Boggess is the author of two books of poetry: *The Prisoners* (Brick Road, 2014) and *The Beautiful Girl Whose Wish Was Not Fulfilled* (Highwire, 2003). His novel, *A Song without a Melody,* is forthcoming from Hyperborea Publishing. His writing has appeared in *Harvard Review, Rattle, River Styx, North Dakota Quarterly,* and many other journals. He lives in Charleston, WV.

Kathleen Sheeder Bonanno's book, *Slamming Open the Door* (Alice James), a memoir in poetry form about the murder of her daughter, was among the ten best-selling books of poetry in the US in 2009. Bonanno has been the Founding Director of Musehouse: A Center for the Literary Arts, in Philadelphia, PA, since 2011. She has work forthcoming in *BOAAT, Kentucky Review,* and *Valparaiso Poetry Review.*

Z. Z. Boone's collection of short stories, *Off Somewhere,* was published in November by Whitepoint Press.

G. F. Boyer is a freelance editor of fiction, creative nonfiction, and poetry, and she's the founder and editor of *Clementine Poetry Journal* and *Clementine (Unbound).* Her poems have appeared in a number of publications, including *The Southern Review, Prairie Schooner, Poetry Northwest, RHINO,* and *Heron Tree.*

Jesse Breite's recent poetry has appeared in *Tar River Poetry, Chiron Review,* and *Prairie Schooner.* He has been featured in *Town Creek Poetry and The Southern Poetry Anthology, Volume V: Georgia.* FutureCycle Press published his first chapbook, *The Knife Collector,* in November 2013.

Kristene Brown is a psychiatric social worker for the State of Kansas. Her poetry and fiction has previously been published in *The Cortland Review, Midwest Quarterly, Linebreak, Jabberwock, upstreet,* and others. Kristene lives and works in Kansas City.

Jeff Burt lives in California with his wife amid the redwoods and two-lane roads wide enough for one car. He has work in *The Nervous Breakdown, Amarillo Bay, Atticus Review,* and forthcoming in *Per Contra*. He was the featured summer issue poet of *Clerestory,* won the 2011 SuRaa short fiction award, and been nominated for a Best of the Net Award.

Elizabeth Burton lives with her husband and two willful dogs in Lexington, KY, where she works for a nonprofit. She is writing furiously on her first book, a collection of short stories about the Uyghur people of Northwest China. "The Curse of Mao" is part of that collection.

Roger Camp lives in Seal Beach, CA, where he gardens, walks the pier, travels the Old World, plays blues piano and spends afternoons with his pal, Harry, over drinks at Nick's on 2nd.

Jessie Carty is the author of seven poetry collections, which includes the chapbook *An Amateur Marriage* (Finishing Line, 2012), a finalist for the 2011 Robert Watson Prize, and her newest full-length collection, *Practicing Disaster,* which was published by Aldrich Press in 2014.

Kevin Casey's work is forthcoming or has appeared recently in *Paper Nautilus, Green Hills Literary Lantern, Rust+Moth, San Pedro River Review,* and other publications. His chapbook, *The Wind Considers Everything,* was recently published by Flutter Press, and another from Red Dashboard is due out later this year.

Alan Catlin's latest full-length book is *Last Man Standing* from Lummox Press. Forthcoming, *American Odyssey,* from FutureCycle Press.

Yu-Han (Eugenia) Chao was born and grew up in Taipei, Taiwan. She received her BA from National Taiwan University and MFA from Penn State. The Backwaters Press published her poetry book, *We Grow Old*. Dancing girl press, Imaginary Friend Press, and BOAAT Press published her chapbooks. Her short story collection, *Sex and Taipei City,* is forthcoming with Red Hen Press.

C. M. Chapman is a graduate of the low-residency MFA program at West Virginia Wesleyan College, where he is the McKinney Teaching Fellow for 2015-16. His work has appeared in *Cheat River Review, Dark Mountain* in the UK, and the anthology, *So It Goes: A Tribute to Kurt Vonnegut*. He was a finalist in the 2015 Curt Johnson Prose Awards. "Blood" is a part of his yet-unpublished thesis collection, *Suicidal Gods*.

Kelly Cherry has recently published *Twelve Women in a Country Called America: Stories* (Press 53); *A Kelly Cherry Reader* (SFASUP); *A Kind of Dream: Stories* (U of Wisconsin); and a poetry chapbook titled *Physics for Poets* (Unicorn Press). A new full-length collection of poems is forthcoming from L.S.U. Press in 2017.

Michael Chin was born and raised in Utica, NY, and currently writes and teaches in Corvallis, OR. He won the 2014 Jim Knudsen Editor's Prize for fiction from the University of New Orleans and has previously published fiction and poetry in over 20 journals, including *Bayou Magazine, The Rappahannock Review,* and *The Pacific Review*. Find him online at miketchin.com and follow him on Twitter @miketchin.

David Chorlton was born in Austria, grew up in Manchester, England, and lived for several years in Vienna before moving to Phoenix in 1978. Arizona's landscapes and wildlife have become increasingly important to him and a significant part of his poetry. Meanwhile, he retains an appetite for reading Eugenio Montale, W. S. Merwin, Tomas Tranströmer and many other, often less celebrated, poets.

Joan Colby has published widely in journals such as *Poetry, Atlanta Review, South Dakota Review,* etc. Awards include two Illinois Arts Council Literary Awards and an Illinois Arts Council Fellowship in Literature. She has published 16 books, including *Selected Poems* from FutureCycle Press, which received the 2013 FutureCycle Prize, and *Ribcage* from Glass Lyre Press, which was awarded the 2015 Kithara Book Prize. Colby is also a senior editor of FutureCycle Press and an associate editor of *Kentucky Review.*

Douglas Cole has published three poetry collections, *Interstate* (Night Ballet Press), *Western Dream* (Finishing Line Press), and *The Dice Throwers* (Liquid Light Press), as well as a novella, *Ghost* (Blue Cubicle Press). His work has appeared in anthologies such as *Best New Writing* (Hopewell Publications), *Bully Anthology* (Kentucky Stories Press) and *Coming Off the Line* (Main Street Rag Publishing). He also has work in or forthcoming in journals such as *The Chicago Quarterly Review, Chiron, Iconoclast, Slipstream, San Pedro River Review, Edge, Solstice* and *The Ocean State Review,* as well as recorded stories in *Bound Off* and *The Baltimore Review.* He is currently on the faculty at Seattle Central College. Check out his website: douglastcole.com.

Ed Coletti is a poet, painter, fiction writer, and chess player who studied under Robert Creeley in San Francisco (1970-71). Ed recently has had work in *The Brooklyn Rail, North American Review, Big Bridge, Hawai'i Pacific Review, Spillway, Lilliput Review,* and *So It Goes—The Literary Journal of the Kurt Vonnegut Memorial Library.* Internet presence includes his popular blog, *No Money In Poetry.* Coletti's book, *When Hearts Outlive Minds,* was released June 2011. *Germs, Viruses, and Catechisms* was published by *Civil Defense Publications* (San Francisco) during Winter 2013. *The Problem With Breathing* from Edwin E. Smith Publications (Little Rock) was published during June 2015. *Apollo Blue's Harp,* a poetic history of music, will also be published by Edwin E. Smith in 2016.

Despite loving all sports, **David Colodney** realized at an early age that he had no athletic ability whatsoever, so he decided to focus his attention on writing about sports instead, covering everything from major league baseball to high school flag football for *The Miami Herald* and *The Tampa Tribune.* Turning to more literary pursuits, David holds an MFA from Converse College, an MA from Nova Southeastern University, and previously served as Poetry Editor of the *South85* literary magazine. His poetry has appeared in *Gyroscope Review, Kentucky Review, Shot Glass Journal,* and *Night Owl.* David lives in Boynton Beach, FL, with his wife, three sons, and golden retriever.

Gayle Compton doesn't give a damn about the rich and famous. He writes about the most misunderstood people in America, the common people of Central Appalachia—his people, bare-assed and proud. He is a widely published Pike County, KY, hillbilly.

Nick Conrad's poems continue to appear in a number of national and international journals, most recently the Fall 2014 issues of *Orbis* (UK), no.168, *Southern Poetry Review,* vol.52, no.2, the 2015 issue of *Blast Furnace,* vol. 5, no.2, and the September 2015 issue of *Hawai'i Pacific Review.* Recently accepted work will be appearing soon in *Badlands.* Other journal publications include *Birmingham Poetry Review, Borderlands, Crab Creek Review, Eclipse, The Literary Review, Magma* (UK), *Orbis* (UK), *The Seattle Review, The Sow's Ear Poetry Review, Stand* (UK), *Texas Literary Review, The Times Literary Supplement* (TLS), *Wisconsin Review,* and others. His poems have been favorably mentioned in online sites like *Verse Daily,* newpages.com, and *Valparaiso Poetry Review.* His work has been included in various anthologies.

J. L. Cooper is a writer and clinical psychologist in Sacramento, CA. His short stories and poetry have appeared or are forthcoming in *The Manhattan Review, Oberon Poetry Magazine, Paper Swans Press, Gold Man Review, KY Story, Temenos Journal, The Sun* (Reader's Write), and in other journals and anthologies. He was recently selected by Adam Johnson as winner of the 2015 *Tupelo Quarterly* prose open prize. Other awards include First Place in Short Short Fiction in New Millennium Writings, 2013, and Second Place in Essay in Literal Latte, 2014.

Ken Craft is a writer and teacher living west of Boston.

Barbara Crooker is the author of six books of poetry: *Radiance,* winner of the 2005 Word Press First Book Award and finalist for the 2006 Paterson Poetry Prize; *Line Dance* (2008), winner of the 2009 Paterson Award for Excellence in Literature; *More* (2010); *Gold* (2013); *Small Rain* (2014); and *Barbara Crooker: Selected Poems* (2015). Her writing has received a number of awards, including the 2004 WB Yeats Society of New York Award, the 2003 Thomas Merton Poetry of the Sacred Award, and three Pennsylvania Council on the Arts Creative Writing Fellowships. Garrison Keillor has read 29 of her poems on *The Writer's Almanac,* and she has read her poetry all over the country, from Portland, OR, to Portland, ME.

Dede Cummings' poetry has been published in *Mademoiselle, The Lake, InQuire,* Vending Machine Press and Connotation Press. She was a Discover/The Nation poetry semi-finalist. She started her publishing career at Little, Brown after graduating from Middlebury College, where she was the recipient of the Mary Dunning Thwing Award for poetry, and in 1991 studied with Hayden Carruth at the Bennington Writers' Workshop. She was a poetry contributor at the Bread Loaf Writers' Conference in 2013 and is currently at work on her first poetry collection and a creative nonfiction called *Spin Cycle.* She lives in West Brattleboro, VT, with her family, where she runs a home office for the publishing company Green Writers Press.

Jim Daniels' latest books are *Rowing Inland,* Wayne State University Press; *Apology to the Moon,* BatCat Press; *Eight Mile High,* stories, Michigan State University Press; and *Birth Marks,* poems. He is the writer/producer of a number of short films, including *The End of Blessings.* Daniels is the Thomas Stockham Baker University Professor at Carnegie Mellon University.

Jim Davis is a student of Human Development and Psychology at Harvard University and has previously studied at Northwestern University and Knox College. He reads for *TriQuarterly* and his work has appeared in *Seneca Review, The Portland Review, Midwest Quarterly,* and *California Journal of Poetics,* among others. He has received multiple Pushcart Prize and Best of the Net nominations and won many contests, including the Line Zero Poetry Prize. In addition to writing and painting, Jim is an international semi-professional American football player. @JimDavisArt

John Davis is the author of *Gigs* and *The Reservist*. His work has appeared recently in *DMQ Review, Iron Horse Literary Review, One,* and *Rio Grande Review*. He lives on an island near Seattle, teaches high school and performs in rock 'n' roll bands.

John Davis Jr. is the author of *Middle Class American Proverb* (Negative Capability Press, 2014). His work has been featured in literary journals and venues internationally, and he has received several Pushcart Prize nominations. He holds an MFA from the University of Tampa.

Gen Del Raye grew up in Kyoto, Japan, and lived there until he was 18. Currently, he is studying marine biology in Berkeley, CA. His stories can be found in *The Monarch Review, Storm Cellar,* and *Corium Magazine*.

William Derge's poems have appeared in *Negative Capability, The Bridge, Artful Dodge, Bellingham Review,* and many other publications. He is the winner of the 2010 Knightsbridge Prize judged by Donald Hall and nominated for a Pushcart Prize. He is a winner of the Rainmaker Award judged by Marge Piercy. He has received honorable mentions in contests sponsored by *The Bridge, Sow's Ear,* and *New Millennium,* among others. He has been awarded a grant by the Maryland State Arts Council.

Lynn DeTurk began studying poetry in 2010 and achieved modest success. In 2012, she won the Writers' Workshop of Asheville poetry and prose contests and quit writing until this year. Recent acceptances are the *Walt Whitman Birthplace Anthology,* Silver Birch Press' *I Am Waiting Series,* and *The Lost Coast Review*.

Benjamin DeVos is an interdisciplinary artist from Philadelphia, studying as a creative writing student at Temple University. His work is published or forthcoming in *Black Denim Lit, Bop Dead City, Pantheon,* and *WhiskeyPaper,* among others.

Heather Dorn has taught poetry for children, teens, adults, and senior citizens in the community as well as a variety of college level writing courses. Her poems have appeared in the *Patterson Literary Review, Ragazine, Metonym, Not One of Us,* and similar journals.

A native of Virginia's Blue Ridge Mountains, **Michael Dowdy** teaches at Hunter College in New York City. His publications include a chapbook, *The Coriolis Effect,* and a study of Latino poetry, *Broken Souths: Latina/o Poetic Responses to Neoliberalism and Globalization*.

Phillip T. Egelston is Advisor on Creative Writing and Visual Arts to the Shawnee Hills Arts Council in Southern Illinois. He is the author of *Reste Placide,* a volume of short lyrical verse, and of the chapbook, *A Liberal Education and Other Poems*.

Brian Fanelli is the author of two poetry books, *Front Man* and *All That Remains*. His third, *Waiting for the Dead to Speak,* is forthcoming from NYQ Books. His poetry, essays, and book reviews have been published by *The Los Angeles Times, World Literature Today, The Paterson Literary Review, [PANK], Main Street Rag,* and elsewhere. He has an MFA from Wilkes University and a PhD from Binghamton University. He teaches at Lackawanna College.

Amy Fant's work has appeared or is forthcoming in *Quaint Magazine, Swarm Literary Journal, Weave, Liminality, Nashville Review,* and *Fiction Southeast,* among others. She's originally from South Carolina, finished her MFA at Emerson College in Boston, and is currently writing and eating her way through Cape Town, South Africa.

Andrea Fekete has one published novel, *Waters Run Wild* (Sweetgum Press 2010) and one poetry chapbook, *I Held a Morning* (Finishing Line Press 2012). Her work has appeared in many journals, such as *Borderlands: Texas Poetry Review, Montucky Review, ABZ,* and *The Adirondack Review,* among many others.

Jenny Ferguson is a Canadian studying for her PhD at the University of South Dakota. Her first novel, *Border Markers,* is forthcoming from NeWest Press.

Rupert Fike's collection of poems, *Lotus Buffet* (Brick Road Poetry Press) was named Finalist in the Georgia Author of the Year awards, 2011. He received Honorable Mention in the 2015 Ron Rash Fiction Award. He has Pushcart Prize nominations in fiction and poetry with work appearing in *The Southern Review of Poetry, Natural Bridge, A & U America's AIDS Magazine, The Buddhist Poetry Review,* and others. He has a poem inscribed in a downtown Atlanta plaza, and his non-fiction book, *Voices from The Farm,* is now in its second printing with accounts of life on a spiritual community in Tennessee.

Colon Foxworth is a former trial lawyer and sports fanatic who hopes to combine his meager literary talent with an earnestness for writing that may result in something that piques the interest of the reader, if not stir her soul. He resides in Middle America, both literally and figuratively.

Katherine Frain is the current poetry editor for *The Blueshift Journal.* Her work has been recognized by the Poetry Society of London, the University of South Carolina, and more, and her works can be found or are forthcoming in *Sugared Water, Spry,* and *burntdistrict.*

Marc Frazier has been widely published in journals including *The Spoon River Poetry Review, ACM, Good Men Project, f(r)iction, Slant, Permafrost, Plainsongs, Poet Lore, Rhino, Wilderness House Literary Review, Connotation Press,* and *Kentucky Review.* He is the recipient of an Illinois Arts Council Award for poetry. His book, *The Way Here,* and his chapbooks, *The Gods of the Grand Resort and After,* are available on Amazon, as well as his second full-length collection, *Each Thing Touches,* from Glass Lyre Press. He had done readings and led workshops in the Chicago area for many years.

D. Dina Friedman has published in numerous literary journals including *Calyx, Common Ground Review, Bloodroot, Inkwell, Pacific Poetry and Fiction Review, Tsunami, The Sun, Anderbo, Rhino,* and *San Pedro River Review,* and she has received two Pushcart Prize nominations. Dina is also the author of two young adult novels, *Escaping Into the Night* and *Playing Dad's Song.* She is in the MFA program at Lesley University and teaches at the University of Massachusetts/Amherst. Visit her website at ddinafriedman.com.

Trevor Fuller is currently an MFA candidate in fiction at Wichita State University and Assistant Editor of *mojo.* His work has appeared or is forthcoming in *Wigleaf: (very) short fiction, Vinyl Poetry, Burningword,* and *Rainy Day.*

Jeannine Hall Gailey served as Redmond, Washington's second Poet Laureate. She's the author of five books of poetry: *Becoming the Villainess, She Returns to the Floating World, Unexplained Fevers, The Robot Scientist's Daughter,* and the upcoming *Field Guide to the End of the World,* winner of the Moon City Press Book Prize. Her work has been featured on NPR's *The Writer's Almanac, Verse Daily,* and in *The Year's Best Fantasy and Horror.*

Armando Jaramillo Garcia was born in Colombia, South America, and raised in New York City. He attended Hunter College and currently works as a photo industry professional at a science and medical agency. He has published recently or is forthcoming in *The Boston Review, Prelude, Horse Less Review, TYPO, Queen Mob's Teahouse,* and others.

Michael Gaspeny has won the Randall Jarrell Poetry Prize and the O. Henry Festival Short Story Competition. His work has appeared in many places, including *Brilliant Corners: A Journal of Jazz and Literature, Cave Wall, Kakalak,* and *Iodine Poetry Journal.* Gaspeny, who lives in Greensboro, NC, taught English and journalism for almost four decades, mainly at Bennett College and High Point University. He was a sportswriter and reporter for several papers in Arkansas; his coverage of Bill Clinton's first campaign for national office is often quoted in biographies of the former president. A hospice volunteer for 13 years, he has received The North Carolina Governor's Award for Volunteer Excellence.

Karen George, author of *Into the Heartland* (Finishing Line Press, 2011), *Inner Passage* (Red Bird Chapbooks, 2014), *Swim Your Way Back* (Dos Madres Press, 2014), *The Seed of Me* (Finishing Line Press, 2015), and *The Fire Circle* (Blue Lyra Press, 2016), has work published in *Naugatuck River Review, Adirondack Review, Louisville Review, Memoir,* and *Still.* She's received grants from Kentucky Foundation for Women and Kentucky Arts Council, holds an MFA in Writing from Spalding University, and is co-founder and fiction editor of the online journal, *Waypoints.*

Joe Giordano was born in Brooklyn. He and his wife, Jane, have lived in Greece, Brazil, Belgium, and The Netherlands. They now live in Texas with their little shih tzu, Sophia. Joe's stories have appeared in more than 70 magazines, including *Bartleby Snopes, The Monarch Review, decomP,* and *Shenandoah.* His novel, *Birds of Passage, An Italian Immigrant Coming of Age Story,* was published by Harvard Square Editions in October 2015. Read the first chapter and sign up for his blog on his website.

Adam Gianforcaro is the author of the poetry collection, *Morning Time in the Household, Looking Out,* and children's picture book, *Uma the Umbrella.* His work can be found in *The Brasilia Review, Hippocampus Magazine, The Los Angeles Review, Sundog Lit,* and others.

After retiring from the Army in 2012, **D. A. Gray** planted roots in Copperas Cove, TX. He now spends his time as a full-time graduate student at Texas A&M-Central Texas in the spring and fall, and as an MFA candidate at Sewanee School of Letters in the summer. Gray has published one book of poetry, *Overwatch,* Grey Sparrow Press, November 2011. His work can be found in *The Sewanee Review, Grey Sparrow Journal, Appalachian Heritage, Still: The Journal, O'Dark Thirty, Kentucky Review, War, Literature and the Arts,* and other literary journals.

Barry Harris is editor of the *Tipton Poetry Journal* and has published one poetry collection, *Something At The Center*. Barry lives in Brownsburg, IN, and is retired from Eli Lilly and Company. His poetry appears in *Grey Sparrow, Silk Road Review, Boston Literary Magazine, Night Train, Cherry Blossom Review, Flying Island, The Centrifugal Eye, Flutter, Wheelhouse Magazine, Houston Literary Review, Snow Monkey, Writers' Bloc,* and others. One of his poems is on display at the National Museum of Sport, and another is painted on a barn in Boone County, IN, as part of Brick Street Poetry's Word Hunger public art project. His poems are anthologized in *From the Edge of the Prairie, Motif 3: All the Livelong Day,* and *Twin Muses: Art and Poetry.*

Matthew Haughton's latest book of poetry is *Stand in the Stillness of Woods*. His chapbook, *Bee-coursing Box,* was nominated for the Weatherford Award for Appalachian Poetry Book of the Year. His poems have appeared in many journals, including *Appalachian Heritage, The Four Way Review, Still, Border Crossing,* and *The Louisville Review*. He is currently a student at the Bread Loaf School of English, where he is on a generous fellowship from the C. E. and S. Foundation. Haughton works as a school teacher in his native Kentucky.

William Ogden Haynes is a poet and author of short fiction from Alabama who was born in Michigan and grew up a military brat. He has published three collections of poetry (*Points of Interest, Uncommon Pursuits,* and *Carvings*) and one book of short stories (*Youthful Indiscretions*), all available on Amazon. Over 120 of his poems and short stories have appeared in literary journals and his work is frequently anthologized.

Dixon Hearne teaches and writes in Louisiana. His work has been twice nominated for the Pushcart Prize and the Hemingway/PEN award. His latest books include *Delta Flats: Stories in the Key of Blues and Hope* (2015), *Plainspeak: New and Selected Poems* (2016), and *From Tickfaw to Shongaloo* (novella, 2015), which was awarded Second Place in the William Faulkner-William Wisdom Competition, judged by Moira Crone. Other work appears in *Tulane Review, Oxford American, Collier's Magazine* (online), *Louisiana Literature,* and elsewhere.

Richard Hedderman is a poet, freelance writer, and museum educator. He earned an MA in Creative Writing at the University of New Hampshire and was a three-time Poetry Fellow at the New York State Writers Institute. His poems appear in *South Dakota Review, CutBank, Chautauqua Literary Review, The Midwest Quarterly, Eclipse, Blue Collar Review, Arsenic Lobster, Negative Capability,* and *Skald* (Wales), among others. His work has also appeared in several anthologies, including *The Anthology of New England Writers* and *In a Fine Frenzy—Poets Respond to Shakespeare* (University of Iowa Press). He authored a poetry collection, *The Discovery of Heaven* (Parallel Press), and was a featured poet at the Library of Congress as part of the *Poetry at Noon* reading series.

Dianna Henning was born and raised in Vermont. She holds an MFA from Vermont College. She received a Pushcart nomination from *Blue Fifth Review* in December 2015 for a flash fiction piece that has also been nominated for the Queens Ferry Press Best Small Fictions 2016 anthology. She's published in numerous literary magazines. Her new book *Cathedral of the Hand,* is due out through Finishing Line Press in February

2016. Her new manuscript, *The Weight of Distance,* is looking for a publisher. Dianna lives in Lassen County on six acres with her husband Kam and her malamute Sakari. She facilitates The Thompson Peak Writers' Workshop.

Gretchen Hodgin was born in South Carolina, but she lives in Maryland now. Her work has appeared in *Gargoyle, Magma Poetry, Tar River Poetry,* and *Rattle,* among others.

David Brendan Hopes is a poet, playwright, and painter living in Asheville, NC.

Paul Hostovsky's eighth book of poetry, *The Bad Guys,* won the FutureCycle Poetry Book Prize for 2015. His poems have won a Pushcart Prize and two Best of the Net awards, and have been featured on *Poetry Daily* and *Verse Daily,* and in *The Writer's Almanac.* He makes his living in Boston as an ASL interpreter and Braille transcriber.

Kurt Hunt is, in no particular order, a father, a lawyer, a husband, a human, and a daydreamer. Sometimes he writes things, but usually he doesn't.

Joseph Hutchison, currently serving as Poet Laureate of Colorado, is the author of 16 collections of poems, including *The Satire Lounge, Marked Men, Thread of the Real,* and *Bed of Coals* (revised edition available from FutureCycle Press). He has also co-edited, with Andrea L. Watson, the FutureCycle Press Good Works anthology, *Malala: Poems for Malala Yousafzai.* In Fall 2016, the book-publishing arm of the New York Quarterly Foundation, NYQ Books, will issue his collection *The World As Is: New & Selected Poems 1972-2015.* He teaches in and directs the Arts & Culture program for the University of Denver's University College and lives with his wife, Iyengar yoga instructor Melody Madonna, in the mountains southwest of Denver.

Ronald Jackson writes stories, poems, and non-fiction. His work has appeared in *Burningword Literary Journal, The Chattahoochee Review, Firewords Quarterly, Iodine Poetry Journal, North Carolina Literary Review, Prime Number Magazine, Tar River Poetry, Vine Leaves Literary Journal,* and other venues. Ronald is currently working on a flash fiction collection, a crime novel set in Philadelphia, his town of origin, and a poetry chapbook. He lives in Durham, NC. Recognitions include honorable mention in the Doris Betts Fiction Prize competition in 2012, third prize in Prime Number Magazine's 2014 flash fiction competition, and honorable mention in the 2014 New Millennium Writings short-short fiction competition.

Mike James has been widely published in magazines throughout the country. He has published seven poetry collections. *Past Due Notices: Poems 1991-2011* (2012, Main Street Rag) and *Elegy in Reverse* (2014, Aldrich Press) are his most recent. A new collection, *The Year We Let the House Fall Down,* was published in September 2015 by Aldrich Press. With his wife, Diane, he is the founder and publisher of Yellow Pepper Press, a small poetry broadside press. After years spent in South Carolina, Missouri, and Pennsylvania, he now lives in North Carolina with his wife and five children.

Susan Johnson's poems have recently appeared in *North American Review, Oyez Review, Off the Coast,* and *SLAB.* She teaches writing at UMass Amherst where she received her PhD in Rhetoric.

George Kalamaras served as Poet Laureate of Indiana (2014-2016) and is the author of 14 books of poetry, seven of which are full-length, including *Kingdom of Throat-Stuck Luck,* winner of the Elixir Press Poetry Prize (2011), and *The Theory and Function of Mangoes,* winner of the Four Way Books Intro Series (2000). He is Professor of English at Indiana University-Purdue University Fort Wayne, where he has taught since 1990.

Susan Doble Kaluza's work has been published or is forthcoming in *Rattle, Eunoia Review,* and others. She has a poetry chapbook, along with new essays, currently out to publishers.

Debra Kaufman is the author *of Delicate Thefts* and *The Next Moment (*both by Jacar Press) and *A Certain Light* (Emrys), as well as three chapbooks. Her poems have appeared most recently in *Poetry East, Spillway,* and *North Carolina Literary Review* and in the anthologies *Intimacy* and *Southern Poetry Anthology.* She is an editor for the online journal *One* and a member of the board of trustees of the Paul Green Foundation.

Ami Kaye is the publisher at Glass Lyre Press and editor of *Pirene's Fountain* and the Aeolian Harp Series. Her poems, reviews, and articles have appeared in various journals and anthologies including *Naugatuck River Review, Levure littéraire, Iodine Poetry Journal, Tiferet, and Cartier Street Review,* among others. Ami edited *Sunrise from Blue Thunder,* and co-edited *First Water: Best of Pirene's Fountain.* She is the author of *What Hands Can Hold* and working on a benefit anthology, *Collateral Damage,* to raise funds for disadvantaged children.

Gloria Keeley is a graduate of San Francisco State University with a BA and MA in Creative Writing. She volunteers at the grammar school she attended, teaching poetry writing to third graders. Her work has appeared in *Spoon River Poetry Review, The MacGuffin, Midnight Circus, Orbis, Stillwater, Ember: A Journal of Luminous Things, El Portal,* and others.

Robert Lee Kendrick lives in Clemson, SC. He has previously published, or has work forthcoming, in *Louisiana Literature, South Carolina Review, The James Dickey Review, Kestrel,* and *Main Street Rag.*

Robert King's first book, *Old Man Laughing* (Ghost Road Press), was a finalist for the 2008 Colorado Book Award in Poetry and his second, *Some of These Days,* appeared in 2013 from Conundrum Press. He lives in Loveland, CO, where he directs the website ColoradoPoetsCenter.org.

Michael Koenig has published stories in recent issues of *The MacGuffin, Harpur Palate, Hardboiled,* and the *Paterson Literary Review.* His work has also been anthologized in *Awake! A Reader for the Sleepless* (Soft Skull Press) and *The Shamus Sampler 2,* an international detective fiction collection.

J. D. Kotzman works in the health policy field and lives in the Washington, DC, area with his girlfriend and two pugs, Grendel and Ginger. Previously, he has served as an editor and writer for several print and online news publications. His fiction has appeared or is forthcoming in *Crack the Spine, Inscape, Pidgeonholes, Slink Chunk Press, The Speculative Edge, Straylight,* and the *An Unlikely Companion* collection (a project of Spark). Find more of his writing at amazon.com/author/jdkotzman.

Jennifer Lagier has published ten poetry books and in literary magazines. She taught with California Poets in the Schools and is now a retired college librarian/instructor, member of the Italian American Writers Association, co-edits the *Homestead Review,* and helps coordinate monthly Monterey Bay Poetry Consortium Second Sunday readings. Her first full-length book, *Harbingers,* is forthcoming from Blue Light Press.

Lori Lamothe is the author of two poetry collections, *Trace Elements* and *Happily,* as well as several chapbooks, most recently *Ouija in Suburbia* with dancing girl press. New work appears in *failbetter, The Literary Review, Painted Bride Quarterly, Verse Daily,* and elsewhere.

Rustin Larson's poetry has appeared in *The New Yorker, The Iowa Review, North American Review, Poetry East,* and *The American Entomologist Poet's Guide to the Orders of Insects.* He is the author of *The Wine-Dark House* (Blue Light Press, 2009), *Crazy Star* (selected for the Loess Hills Book's Poetry Series in 2005), *Bum Cantos, Winter Jazz, & The Collected Discography of Morning*, winner of the 2013 Blue Light Book Award (Blue Light Press, San Francisco), and *The Philosopher Savant* (Glass Lyre Press, 2015).

Sean Lause teaches courses in Shakespeare, Literature and the Absurd, and Medical Ethics at Rhodes State College in Lima, OH. His poems have appeared in *The Minnesota Review, The Alaska Quarterly, The Beloit Poetry Journal, The Pedestal, Writer's Journal, Another Chicago Magazine, European Judaism, Sanskrit, Atlanta Review*, and *Poetry International.*

Eleanor Levine's writing has appeared in *Fiction, Evergreen Review, Fiction Southeast, Dos Passos Review, Monkeybicycle, Barely South Review, The Denver Quarterly, Pank, The Toronto Quarterly, Barrelhouse, Intima, Foliate Oak Literary Magazine, Kentucky Review, Juked, The Stockholm Review of Literature, Crack the Spine, Thrice Fiction, Tulane Review* and *The MacGuffin*; forthcoming work in *SRPR (Spoon River Poetry Review)* and *Hobart*. Her short story, The Jew Who Became a Nun," was nominated by *Menacing Hedge* for Best of the Net 2015. Levine's poetry collection, *Waitress at the Red Moon Pizzeria*, will be released by Unsolicited Press in 2016. She is a medical copy editor and lives with her dog in Philadelphia, PA.

Denise H. Long's fiction has appeared in numerous publications, including *Blue Monday Review, Gravel,* and *Burrow Press Review*. In addition to working as a copy editor and fact checker, she also serves as production editor for *Carve* magazine. Denise lives in Nebraska, with her husband and two young sons.

Helen Losse is the author of six collections of poetry. Her latest book *Every Tender Reed* is forthcoming from Main Street Rag in May. Formerly the Poetry Editor for *The Dead Mule*, Helen is an Associate Poetry Editor for *Kentucky Review*.

Denton Loving is the author of the poetry collection *Crimes Against Birds* (Main Street Rag, 2015) and editor of *Seeking Its Own Level*, an anthology of writings about water (MotesBooks, 2014). Follow him on twitter @DentonLoving.

Richard Luftig is a past professor of educational psychology and special education at Miami University in Ohio who now resides in California. He is a recipient of the Cincinnati Post-Corbett Foundation Award for Literature and a semi-finalist for the Emily Dickinson Society Award. His poems have appeared in numerous literary journals in the US, and internationally in Japan, Canada, Australia, Europe, Thailand, Hong Kong, and India. One of his poems was nominated for the 2012 Pushcart Poetry Prize.

Veronica Lupinacci grew up in Sarasota, FL. She received her MFA in creative writing from the University of North Carolina Wilmington. She has served as a founding editor for *Globe's Wing* and an editorial assistant for *Chautauqua*. She has taught writing at the university, high school, middle school, and elementary levels. Her poems have recently appeared in *The McNeese Review, Haiku Journal, The Pinch, Northwind,* and *Eunoia Review.*

Al Maginnes published ten collections of poems, most recently *Music from Small Towns* (Jacar Press, 2014), winner of the annual Jacar Press contest, and *Inventing Constellations* (Cherry Grove Collections, 2012). He has recent or forthcoming work in *Meridian, Southern Review, Cape Rock*, and many others. He lives in Raleigh, NC, and teaches at Wake Technical Community College.

Jennifer Martelli is a graduate of Boston University and The Warren Wilson MFA Program for Writers. Her chapbook, *Apostrophe*, was published in 2011. She is a recipient of the Massachusetts Cultural Council Grant in Poetry, a Pushcart and Best of the Net nominee, and is an associate editor for *The Compassion Project*. She lives in Marblehead, MA, with her family.

A recent graduate of Clemson University's MA in English program, **Joshua Lee Martin** has poems published or forthcoming in *Josephine Quarterly*, *Still*, *Off the Coast, Black Heart Magazine, The San Pedro River Review, Red River Review*, and elsewhere. He is currently working on his first chapbook of poems and plans to attend Georgia State University's PhD program in Creative Writing in the fall.

Poetry can illuminate, electrify. **Jo McCreary** is in it for the ride, chasing that elusive lightning strike. Although most of her work evolves into private conversations between her and poems in progress, she also works with other artists. One of her collaborations, with composer Richard Robinson, is her reading of "Leaving Cumberland" set to music, which appears on his CD, Electroacoustic Music Vol. II., and has been performed in various venues including MOCA GA and the Hambidge Center. She's also worked with artist, Lourdes Perdomo, who applied lines of her text across several of her paintings shown at MOCA.

Matt McGee writes short fiction in the local library until the staff makes him go home. He plays goalie in local hockey leagues and drives around looking to collect characters, stories, and details the way some guys collect classic cars or refrigerator magnets. His story, "Unseen Among Kings," was recently nominated for the Pushcart Award and his collection, *Leaving Rayette*, is available on Amazon.

K. A. McGowan was born and raised in Scranton, PA. His two chapbooks are *Rubric* and *No Passengers*.

Elizabeth McMunn-Tetangco lives in California's Central Valley, where she works as a librarian. Her work has appeared in *The Potomac Review*, *The Más Tequila Review*, *Word Riot*, *Paper Nautilus*, and *Hobart*, among others.

N. T. McQueen is the author of the novel, *Between Lions and Lambs*, *The Disciple*, and the children's book, *Moses Jones and the Case of the Missing Sneaker*. He received his MA in Creative Writing from CSU-Sacramento under the direction of Douglas Rice. He has won two Bazzanella Literary Awards and his work has appeared in issues of *Kentucky Review*, *Gold Man Review*, *Camas: Nature of the West*, *West Trade Review*, *Calliope Magazine,* and others. His book reviews can be found at *Catholic Fiction* and *The Atticus Review*. He lives in Northern California with his wife and three children.

Ken Meisel is a poet and psychotherapist from the Detroit area. He is a 2012 Kresge Arts Literary Fellow, Pushcart Prize nominee, Swan Duckling chapbook contest winner, and author of six poetry collections: *The Drunken Sweetheart at My Door* (FutureCycle Press, 2015), *Scrap Metal Mantra Poems* (Main Street Rag, 2013), *Beautiful Rust* (Bottom Dog Press, 2009), *Just Listening* (Pure Heart Press, 2007), *Before Exiting* (Pure Heart Press, 2006) and *Sometimes the Wind* (March Street Press, 2002). His work is in over 80 national magazines including *Cream City Review*, *Rattle*, *Ruminate*, *Midwest Gothic*, *Concho River Review*, *San Pedro River Review*, *Boxcar Review*, *Lake Effect*, *Birdfeast*, *Muddy River Poetry Review*, *Pirene's Fountain*, *Third Wednesday*, and *Bryant Literary Review*.

Todd Mercer won the Grand Rapids Festival of the Arts Flash Fiction Award for 2015, the first Woodstock Writers Festival Flash Fiction Award, two Kent County Dyer-Ives Poetry Prizes, and was runner-up in the Palm Beach Plein Air Poetry Awards. His digital chapbook, *Life-wish Maintenance*, appeared in 2015 at Right Hand Pointing. Mercer's poetry and fiction appear in journals such as *Apocrypha & Abstractions*, *Cheap Pop*, *Dunes Review*, *Eunoia Review*, *Kentucky Review*, *The Lake*, *The Legendary*, *Literary Orphans*, *Lost Coast Review*, *Main Street Rag Anthologies*, *Midwestern Gothic*, and *Spartan*.

Bryan Merck has published in *Hiram Poetry Review*, *Monarch Review*, *Pleiades*, and elsewhere. His chapbook of poetry, *First Exit*, is available as a download from Triggerfishcriticalreview.com.

Fiction by **Jay Merill** will appear shortly in *Hobart*, *Per Contra*, *Prairie Schooner*, and *tNY Press*. She is a 2017 Pushcart Prize nominee, is the winner of the Salt Short Story Prize, and has two collections published by Salt. Further stories have been published by *Anomalous*, *Epiphany*, *Foliate Oak*, *Ginosko Journal*, *Matter Press*, *SmokeLong Quarterly*, *Wigleaf*, and other great publications.

David Mihalyov lives outside of Rochester, NY, with his wife, two daughters, and two dogs. His poems have appeared in *Concho River Review*, *Free State Review*, *Grey Sparrow Journal*, *Kindred*, *Naugatuck River Review*, and *San Pedro River Review*. He is still waiting for the Chicago Cubs to win a World Series.

Devon Miller-Duggan has published her poetry in *Rattle, Shenandoah, Margie, Christianity and Literature*, and *Gargoyle*. She teaches Creative Writing at the University of Delaware. Her books include *Pinning the Bird to the Wall*, from Tres Chicas Books in 2008, and a chapbook of poems about angels, *Neither Prayer, Nor Bird,* from Finishing Line Press in 2013.

Thomas Mitchell studied writing at Cal State University, Sacramento, where he received his MA, and worked with the poet Dennis Schmitz. He received his MFA in Creative Writing from the University of Montana, where he studied with Richard Hugo. His poems have appeared in numerous journals and anthologies. He taught middle school in Southern Oregon for 31 years, where he lives with his wife Linda. His new book, *The Way Summer Ends*, is forthcoming from Lost Horse Press in the fall of 2016.

Arthur Nahill is an expat American living and writing in New Zealand. His poetry has appeared in print in both hemispheres. His first collection, *A Long Commute Home*, is available online.

Will Nixon's most recent book, *Acrostic Woodstock*, is a town portrait in poems. Previously, he co-authored *The Pocket Guide to Woodstock* and *Walking Woodstock: Journeys into the Wild Heart of America's Most Famous Small Town*. His earlier poetry collections are *My Late Mother as a Ruffed Grouse* and *Love in the City of Grudges*. His website is willnixon.com.

Angie Crea O'Neal is an associate professor at Shorter University in Rome, GA, where she also holds the Joan Alden Speidel Chair in English. Her poems have appeared in *San Pedro River Review* and *The Cumberland River Review*. Her poem, "When the moon tells us of losses," was recently nominated for a Pushcart Prize.

A former US Army interrogator, **Martin Ott** is the author of six books of poetry and fiction, including the poetry book, *Underdays*, Sandeen Prize winner, University of Notre Dame Press, and the short story collection, *Interrogations*, Fomite Press. More at martinottwriter.com.

James Owens' most recent collection of poems is *Mortalia*, from FutureCycle Press.

Elaine Fowler Palencia, a five-time Pushcart Prize nominee, is the author of two short story collections and three poetry chapbooks. The latest chapbook, *Going Places*, was published by FutureCycle Press in 2015. She lives in Champaign, IL, where she is moderator of the Red Herring Fiction Workshop and a member of the Quintessential Poets.

Lee Passarella acts as senior literary editor for *Atlanta Review* magazine. His poetry has appeared in *Chelsea, Cream City Review, Louisville Review, The Formalist, Antietam Review, JAMA, The Wallace Stevens Journal, Cortland Review*, and other periodicals. He has been nominated for two Pushcart Prizes. Passarella has three books of poetry: *Swallowed up in Victory* (Burd Street Press), *The Geometry of Loneliness* (David Robert Books), and *Redemption* (FutureCycle Press). His chapbook, *Sight-Reading Schumann* (Pudding House) will be joined soon by *Magnetic North* (Finishing Line Press). In addition, Passarella has two young-adult novels based on the Civil War: *Storm in the Valley* and *Cold Comfort, Ill Wind* (Ravenswood Publishing).

Tim Peeler's most recent books are *Knuckle Bear* (Red Dirt Press) and *Henry River: An American Ruin* (Lummox Press). He lives in Hickory, NC, where he directs the Learning Assistance Programs at Catawba Valley Community College.

The poetry, fiction, and essays of **Teresa Peipins** have appeared in publications both in the United States and abroad, including *Anak Sastra, Barcelona Ink, The Barcelona Review, The Buffalo News, Conte, Hawai'i Pacific Review, Melusine,* and *Pedestal*, among many others. She is the author of three chapbooks of poetry. Her novel, *The Shadow of Silver Birch*, is published by Black Rose Writing.

Mary Petralia completed an MFA in Creative Writing at the University of Central Florida in December 2015. Her poems have appeared in *Shooter Literary Magazine, London Journal of Fiction, Tincture Journal, Eyedrum Periodically, Anamesa: An Interdisciplinary Journal, Hitherto: The MUIC Literary Journal, Ishaan Literary Review, 99 Pine Street,* and other publications. She lives on the east coast of Florida with her family.

Alice Pettway's work has appeared in over 30 print and online journals, including *The Bitter Oleander, The Connecticut Review, Folio, Keyhole,* and *WomenArts Quarterly*. Her chapbook, *Barbed Wire and Bedclothes*, was published by Spire Press in 2009, and her full-length collection, *The Time of Hunger | O Tempo de Chuva*, is forthcoming from Salmon Poetry. Pettway is a former Lily Peter fellow, Raymond L. Barnes Poetry Award winner, and three-time Pushcart Prize nominee. Currently, she teaches creative writing in Bogotá, Colombia.

Cathy Porter's poetry has appeared in *Plainsongs, Homestead Review, California Quarterly, Chaffin Journal,* and various other publications. She has two chapbooks available from Finishing Line Press. Her newest collection, *Exit Songs*, is forthcoming from dancing girl press. She lives in Omaha, NE.

Steph Post is the author of the novels, *A Tree Born Crooked* and *Lightwood*. She currently lives, writes, and teaches writing in St. Petersburg, FL.

Marjorie Power recently moved to Denver, CO, after many years west of the Cascades. She finds writing poetry not only possible but enjoyable where the weather's default mode is blazing sunshine. Her newest collection, *Seven Parts Woman,* is forthcoming this year from WordTech Editions.

Bill Richter was born and raised in Southern California. He has lived in San Francisco since 1991, where he resides with his wife and their son. HIs fiction has appeared in *So It Goes*, the journal of the Kurt Vonnegut Memorial Library. He has had other work published in the books, *Hungry? San Francisco* and *Thirsty? San Francisco*.

Amy Riddell is the author of *Bullets in the Jewelry Box*, a full-length poetry collection published by FutureCycle Press, and *Narcissistic Injury*, a chapbook published by Pudding House Press. Her poems have appeared in *Prairie Schooner, Black Warrior Review, Birmingham Poetry Review, Prick of the Spindle,* and *Blue Fifth Review,* among other journals.

Ron Riekki's non-fiction, fiction, and poetry have been published in *River Teeth*, *Spillway*, *New Ohio Review*, *Shenandoah*, *Canary*, *Bellevue Literary Review*, *New Orleans Review*, *Prairie Schooner*, *Little Patuxent Review*, *Wigleaf*, and a number of other literary journals.

Marissa Rose's work has previously appeared in print or online with *Breadcrumb Scabs*, *The Lyric*, *Steel Toe Review*, *Camera Obscura*, and *Word Riot*. Find her somewhat reticent blog at marissacoonrose.com, or on Twitter at @mcrose1186.

Rosemary Royston, author of *Splitting the Soil* (Finishing Line Press, 2014), resides in northeast Georgia with her family. Her writing has been published in journals such as *NANO Fiction*, *Appalachian Heritage*, *Southern Poetry Review*, *Town Creek Review*, **82 Review*, and *Razor Literary Magazine*.

Leslie M. Rupracht is the longtime senior associate editor of *Iodine Poetry Journal*. She also spent five years editing prose and photography for *moonShine review*. Her poems, short fiction, creative non-fiction, photos, and other visual art appear in various journals and anthologies. Her poetry chapbook is *Splintered Memories* (Main Street Rag Publishing Company, 2012). A 1997 transplant from New York to North Carolina, Leslie lives near Charlotte with her husband and rescued pit bull. An advocate for the environment and sustainability, Leslie often explores the natural world with her camera. She co-hosts a monthly featured reading and open mic night.

Terry Savoie has had poems published in more than 300 literary journals, including *Poetry*, *Prairie Schooner*, *APR*, *Ploughshares*, *The Iowa Review*, and *The North American Review*.

Jan Zlotnik Schmidt is a SUNY Distinguished Professor of English at SUNY New Paltz, where she teaches composition, creative writing, American and Women's Literature, creative nonfiction, memoir, and Holocaust literature courses. Her work has been published in many journals, including *The Cream City Review*, *Kansas Quarterly*, *The Alaska Quarterly Review*, *Home Planet News*, *Phoebe*, *Black Buzzard Review*, *The Chiron Review*, and *Wind*. Her work also has been nominated for the Pushcart Press Prize Series. She has had two volumes of poetry published by the Edwin Mellen Press (*We Speak in Tongues*, 1991; *She had this memory*, *2000*). Her chapbook, *The Earth Was Still*, was recently published by Finishing Line Press.

Jason Sears is a West Philadelphia poet by way of Louisville, KY. His work appears in *The Monarch Review* and other fine journals. He edits *By&By Poetry* and believes, without reservation, in the redemptive power of a hard day's work.

Dahlia Seroussi is a bilingual poet who hails from the San Francisco Bay Area. She received her BA from the University of California Santa Cruz and is currently pursuing her MFA at Oregon State University. Her poems have appeared in *Eleven Eleven*, *Chinquapin*, and *Monterey Poetry Review*. Her chapbook, *What I Know*, was published by Finishing Line Press in 2013.

Danny Earl Simmons is an Oregonian and a proud graduate of Corvallis High School. He is a friend of the Linn-Benton Community College Poetry Club and currently serves on its Poetry Advisory Committee. His poems have appeared in a variety of journals, such as *The Pedestal Magazine*, *Little Patuxent Review*, *IthacaLit*, *San Pedro River Review*, and *Off the Coast*, where he now assists as a member of the editorial staff.

A graduate of the University of Southern Maine's Stonecoast MFA Poetry Program, **David Sloan** is the author of two books on Waldorf education. His debut poetry collection, *The Irresistible In-Between*, was published by Deerbrook Editions in 2013. His poetry has appeared in *The Café Review*, *Chiron Review*, *Houseboat*, *Innisfree*, *Lascaux Review*, *Maine Review*, *Naugatuck River Review*, *New Millennium Writings*, and *Passager*, among others. He received the 2012 Betsy Sholl and Maine Literary awards, and has been nominated for a Pushcart Prize. He is currently enjoying life's latest delight—grandfatherhood!

Ian C. Smith's work has appeared in *Australian Poetry Journal*, *New Contrast*, *Poetry Salzburg Review*, *Rabbit Journal*, *The Stony Thursday Book*, *Two-Thirds North*, and *Westerly*. His seventh book is *wonder sadness madness joy*, Ginninderra (Port Adelaide). He lives in the Gippsland Lakes area of Victoria, Australia.

Ronnie K. Stephens is a full-time English teacher and the father of identical twins. His poems often explore vulnerability in its many facets. His first collection, *Universe in the Key of Matryoshka*, was published by Timber Mouse Publishing in 2014. Individual poems have previously appeared or are forthcoming in *Rattle*, *Paper Nautilus*, *Weave*, and *Union Station*, among others.

Anders M. Svenning lives in South Florida. His work has appeared in *Forge Journal*, *Grey Sparrow Journal*, and many more. His work is forthcoming in *Bahamut Journal*. His motto: What seems evident rarely is the case.

Wally Swist's books include *Huang Po and the Dimensions of Love* (Southern Illinois University Press, 2012); *The Daodejing: A New Interpretation*, with David Breeden and Steven Schroeder (Lamar University Literary Press, 2015); and *Invocation* (Lamar University Literary Press, 2015). His poems have appeared in many publications, including *Commonweal*, *North American Review*, *Sunken Garden Poetry, 1992-2011* (Wesleyan University Press, 2012), and *upstreet*. Garrison Keillor recently read a poem of Swist's on *The Writer's Almanac*.

Mark Taksa's poems are appearing in *Texas Review*, *Blue Unicorn*, and *Third Wednesday*. He is the author of ten chapbooks. *The Invention of Love* (March Street Press), *Love Among the Antiquarians* (Pudding House), and *The Torah at the End of the Train* (Poetica Magazine) are the most recent.

Dylan Taylor is a university drop-out who slings cheap coffee to cottagers and builds dry stone walls in Canada. When he's not working, he's spending his wages on tickets to Virginia to see his fiancé and Emerson, the best duo on the continent. He has work published in *Blotterature*, *The Lost Country*, and *decomP*.

George Thompson is a Kentucky native who divides his time between corporate drudgery, husbandry, and compromised artistry. Most of his writing is created in the lulls of late evenings and very early mornings. George's work is largely reflective and evaluative, seeking meaning from small experiences. He most recently placed two pieces with the Kentucky State Poetry Society and received mention on two others.

Michael Tugendhat has an MLitt in creative writing, and will be pursuing an MFA in the summer. He was a member of the Curtis Brown Creative course, and has a chapbook releasing with Five Oaks Press.

Jay Udall teaches at Nicholls State University in Thibodaux, LA, where he serves as poet-in-residence and chief editor of the online journal, *Gris-Gris*. More at jayudall.net.

Milla van der Have (1975) wrote her first poem at 16, during a physics class. She has been writing ever since. One of her short stories has won a New Millennium Fiction Award. In 2015, she published a book of poems about Virginia City, Nevada. Milla lives and works in Utrecht, The Netherlands.

Donna Vitucci is Development Director of Covington Ladies Home, the only free-standing personal care home exclusively for elderly women in Northern Kentucky. Her stories have appeared in dozens of print and online journals, including *PANK*, *Fifth Wednesday Journal*, *Gargoyle*, *Hinchas de Poesia*, *Contrary*, *Corium*, *Southern Women's Review*, *Change Seven*, and *The Butter*. Her novel, *At Bobby Trivette's Grave*, will be published by Rebel E Press in 2016. Her unpublished novel, *Feed Materials*, was a finalist for the Bellwether Prize and waits with other finished novels in a trunk. (Yes, a real old-timey trunk!)

Elizabeth Kirkpatrick Vrenios is professor emerita from American University, having chaired the vocal and music departments. Vrenios' solo recitals throughout the US, South America, Scandinavia, Japan, and Europe have been acclaimed. Recently featured in Tupelo Press's 30/30 challenge, she has been published in *Clementine*, *Poeming Pigeon*, *Crack the Spine*, *Cumberland River Review*, *The Feminine Collective*, and *Edison Literary Review*. Her chapbook, *unraveled*, won second prize in the Yellow Chair Press Competition, and will be forthcoming in the spring. As the artistic director of the Redwoods Opera in Mendocino, California, and the Crittenden Opera Workshop in Washington, DC, and Boston, she has influenced and trained vocal students across the country.

Connemara Wadsworth's chapbook, *The Possibility of Scorpions*, won the White Eagle Coffee Store Press 2009 Chapbook Contest and is about the years her family lived in Baghdad, Iraq, in the early 1950s. Her work has been published in magazines such as *Bloodroot Literary Magazine*, *Colere*, *Comstock Review*, *Connecticut River Review*, *Ibbetson Street*, *Northern New England Review*, *Off the Coast*, *Poet Lore*, and *Pudding Review*, and in the anthology, *Passionate Hearts*, by Wendy Maltz. "The Women," published in *Bloodroot Magazine*, was nominated for a Pushcart Prize in the Best of the Small Presses.

Robert Walicki's debut chapbook is *A Room Full of Trees* (Redbird Press). His work has appeared in numerous journals, including *Stone Highway Review*, *Pittsburgh City Paper*, and *The Pittsburgh Post-Gazette*, and on the radio show, *Prosody*. His next chapbook, *The Almost Sound of Snow Falling*, is forthcoming this winter from Night Ballet Press.

Court Walsh taught public school for almost 30 years, retired, and started writing fiction. So far, he has published a dozen stories. Just about every day, he takes his dog Snooker out on his foldable terra-trike. By the end of this week, he will have logged 1,000 miles.

Lisa Weiss is a seasoned concert pianist and the Todd Distinguished Professor of Music at Goucher College in Baltimore, MD. She made her solo debut with the Boston Pops at age seven, performing a Haydn concerto. She earned her BA in music from Harvard University, MMA from the Yale School of Music, DMA from the Peabody Conservatory, and MMA in Creative Writing-Fiction from Lesley University. She has completed one short story collection and is working on her second. Her extended essay, *Reflections on the Revision Process by a Classical Pianist,* parallels the worlds of writing, art, musical composition, and musical performance. Her husband is the painter Howie Lee Weiss. Their son, Billie, is a photojournalist for the Boston Red Sox.

Now retired from her career as a college administrator and communications professor, **Jill White** has become an award-winning jewelry artist and poet. Her poetry has appeared in numerous literary journals, including *Kentucky Review, U.S. 1 Worksheets, The Poetry Quarterly, Olentangy Review,* and *Cumberland River Review.*

Pediatrician **Kelley White** worked in inner city Philadelphia and now works in rural New Hampshire. Her poems have appeared in journals including *Exquisite Corpse, Rattle,* and *JAMA.* Her most recent books are *Toxic Environment* (Boston Poet Press) and *Two Birds in Flame* (Beech River Books.) She received a 2008 Pennsylvania Council on the Arts grant.

Harold Whit Williams is guitarist for the Austin-based rock band, Cotton Mather. Recipient of the 2014 Mississippi Review Poetry Prize and a featured poet in the 2014 University of North Texas Kraken Reading Series, his collection, *Backmasking,* was winner of the 2013 Robert Phillips Poetry Chapbook Prize from Texas Review Press. His latest collection of poems, *Lost in the Telling,* is available from FutureCycle Press.

Martin Willitts Jr. has published 28 chapbooks, including national chapbook contest-winning *William Blake, Not Blessed Angel But Restless Man* (Red Ochre Press, 2014. He has seven full-length collections including national award winner *Searching for What You Cannot See* (Hiraeth Press, 2013). Other collections are forthcoming from UNBOUND Content, Kattywompus Press, Writing Knights Press, and FutureCycle Press. In 2014, Martin won the Dylan Thomas International Poetry Contest, and several of his poems in this issue are based on his visit to Swansea, Wales, to receive the award and read his poems.

Jenni Wiltz holds an MA in creative writing from California State University, Sacramento, where she won three Bazzanella Literary Awards in fiction and critical analysis. Her work has appeared in *Gargoyle, The Portland Review, Sacramento News & Review,* and several small-press anthologies. When she's not writing, she enjoys sewing, running, and genealogical research. She lives in Pilot Hill, CA.

Pete Wingard is currently a web developer at The Weather Channel. When he isn't writing hot, bright, and sunny code in Atlanta, he writes somewhat cold and cloudy poetry. He has been published in *Slant: a Journal of Poetry* and *Negative Capability Press.*

Shannon K. Winston is currently a Postdoctoral Lecturer in Princeton University's Writing Program. She is also a translator, poet, and poetry critic. Her work has appeared in several journals, including *Absinthe: A Journal of World Literature in Translation*, *Gingerbread House*, and *Zone 3*. Her first full-length poetry collection, *Threads Give Way* (Cold Press), was published in 2010. She is currently pursuing her MFA at Warren Wilson College.

Guinotte Wise wrote a book of short stories, *Night Train, Cold Beer*, at his farm in Resume Speed, KS, where he welds and writes. It won and got published, to not much acclaim. It's on Amazon. He got the soffits fixed with the money. Black Opal Books published his next book, *Ruined Days*, a thriller also on Amazon and other booksellers. A second collection of short stories, *Resume Speed*, is in final edits. His stories have appeared in numerous literary reviews, including *Atticus*, *The MacGuffin*, *Shotgun Honey*, and *Best New Writers Anthology 2015*. His wife has an honest job in the city and drives 100 miles a day to keep it.

Francine Witte is the author of the poetry chapbooks *Only, Not Only* (Finishing Line Press, 2012) and *First Rain* (Pecan Grove Press, 2009), winner of the Pecan Grove Press competition. Her flash fiction chapbook are *Cold June* (Ropewalk Press), selected by Robert Olen Butler as the winner of the 2010 Thomas A. Wilhelmus Award; and *The Wind Twirls Everything* (MuscleHead Press). A former English teacher, Francine lives in New York.

Gerald Yelle's book of poems, *The Holyoke Diaries*, was published by FutureCycle Press. A dime flash novel, *Evolution for the Hell of It*, was published by Red Dashboard Press. He teaches high school English and is a member of the Florence (MA) Poets Society.

About Kentucky Review

Kentucky Review, based in Lexington, was founded in 2014 as both an online and a print publication. Poems and flash fiction are published on our website throughout the year and then gathered into an annual print edition published in the first quarter of the following year. As part of FutureCycle Press's Good Works projects, proceeds from donations and sales of the printed edition of KR are donated to Action Against Hunger.

KR is always open to submissions via our online system (Submittable). Please see the guidelines at www.kentuckyreview.net before submitting. We do not charge reading fees but have an option for small donations that are also given to charity.

We do not publish theme issues. We like variety in subject and style and welcome your submissions.